M000301961

'A brilliantly readable account of the remarkable Josephine Butler, who turned the Victorian patriarchy on its head and changed the world for women at immense personal cost. If there is a canon of feminist heroines, Butler should be right at the top.'
Daisy Goodwin, novelist, screenwriter and author of *Victoria*

'In this brief history, Jane Robinson outlines the fascinating contradictions – and extraordinary achievements – of a great Victorian social reformer. Josephine Butler challenged the contempt levelled at women who sold sex, and the unjust laws passed and enforced by men to punish them. Sharp, authoritative and eye-opening.'
Helen Lewis, journalist and author of *Difficult Women: A History of Feminism in 11 Fights*

'This is an important book about a social reformer of the Victorian era in danger of being forgotten. Jane Robinson brings Josephine Butler to life, highlighting how she came to take up a range of causes, how she successfully challenged social norms and laws - particularly the double standards around prostitution. A story of a woman who defied what was expected of her to make a difference – told in a wonderfully engaging way.'
Helen Pankhurst, author of *Deeds not Words: The Story of Women's Rights Then and Now*

JOSEPHINE BUTLER

A very brief history

Jane Robinson

First published in Great Britain in 2020

Society for Promoting Christian Knowledge
36 Causton Street
London SW1P 4ST
www.spck.org.uk

Copyright © Jane Robinson 2020

All rights reserved. No part of this book may be reproduced or transmitted in any form
or by any means, electronic or mechanical, including photocopying, recording, or by any
information storage and retrieval system, without permission in writing from the publisher.

SPCK does not necessarily endorse the individual views contained in its publications.

Unless otherwise noted, Scripture quotations are taken from The King James Bible,
the rights in which are vested in the Crown, and is reproduced by permission
of the Crown's Patentee, Cambridge University Press.

British Library Cataloguing-in-Publication Data
A catalogue record for this book is available from the British Library

ISBN 978–0–281–08062–5
eBook ISBN 978–0–281–08063–2

1 3 5 7 9 10 8 6 4 2

Typeset by Nord Compo
Printed and bound in Great Britain by TJ Books Limited

eBook by Nord Compo

Produced on paper from sustainable forests

To Richard

Contents

Acknowledgements

A good deal of careful scholarship surrounds the facts of Josephine Butler's life and I'm grateful to everyone who shared their expertise and enthusiasm with me in conversation, in print, and in libraries and archives around the country. Excerpts in the book are reproduced with the kind permission of Special Collections, Leeds University Library; the University of Liverpool Library; Northumberland Archives, and the Women's Library at the LSE. My thanks to staff there and at the Bodleian Libraries in Oxford for their patient help. Special mention must go to Claire Grey for her generosity in allowing me access to material relating to the Grey and Butler families.

Personal touches mean a lot during research. Ian Kille welcomed me to Kirknewton and showed me around the village church that meant so much to Josephine, while friends on Twitter readily responded to my request for current awareness of Josephine and her work. The encouragement of my agent, Véronique Baxter; the professionalism of my editor at SPCK, Philip Law, and the boundless support of my family, are all much appreciated.

Finally, a word for my dedicatee. Our son, Dr Richard James, works in public health – as did Josephine Butler. I'm beyond proud of what he does, and who he is.

Jane Robinson.

Chronology

1828 Born Josephine Elizabeth Grey on 13 April at Milfield, Northumberland.

1852 Marries academic and cleric George Butler; settles in Oxford. Their four children are born in 1852 (George), 1854 (Stanley), 1856 (Charles) and 1859 (Eva).

1857 Moves to Cheltenham on account of her ill health.

1861 Outbreak of American Civil War. Ostracized for her support of the Unionists.

1864 Daughter Eva is killed by a fall. First Contagious Diseases Act (CDA) is passed; two more follow in 1866 and 1869.

1866 Moves to Liverpool and begins activism against CDAs. Signs John Stuart Mill's Women's Suffrage petition to Parliament.

1867 Takes former prostitutes into her home and opens a hostel for them. Appointed president of North of England Council for Promoting the Cause of Higher Education for Women.

1868 Joins Married Women's Property Committee.

1869 Appointed Hon. Sec. of Ladies' National Association for the Repeal of the Contagious Diseases Acts (LNA).

1871 Gives evidence to Royal Commission on the operation of the CDAs.

1874 First campaign tour of Continent.

1880   Begins campaigning against white slave trade in Britain and the Continent.

1882   Moves to Winchester. Married Women's Property Act is passed.

1885   W. T. Stead publishes *Maiden Tribute of Modern Babylon* exposing the sale of young women into prostitution. Butler speaks at his subsequent trial. Age of consent raised from 13 to 16.

1886   Repeal of CDAs. Turns her attention to state regulation of vice in British India.

1890   Death of George Butler.

1906   Dies in Wooler, Northumberland, on 30 December.

Part 1

THE HISTORY

1

Designed for happiness

It can seem at times that nineteenth-century Britain was peopled entirely by stereotypes. Think of a Victorian gentleman: he wears a top hat and stiff collar, has extravagant whiskers and carries a cane. All day he sits in a vast mahogany office, where banks of shirt-sleeved clerks endlessly transcribe documents in the background. His porcelain wife is installed in their suburban villa or place in the country, her stays too tightly laced for her to move – an innocent 'angel in the house' of whom nothing more is required than a devotion to domestic duty.

Meanwhile the lower classes work industriously, grateful to keep their heads above water. Down in the depths, the poor struggle desperately to survive: that is their lot in life. There is a middle class of men who make their way in the world by means of art, literature, science or religion and a corresponding class of frustrated women whose only chance of prosperity is to marry well. Once married, they are safe. Impotent, but safe. This is the Dickensian, Brontë-esque world in which Josephine Butler spent most of her life. In our reductive hindsight, it is a world of caricature. Yet that is how it also appeared to many who lived through it: a society governed by clearly defined boundaries and roles, where success meant doing exactly what was expected.

Josephine Elizabeth Grey was born on 13 April 1828 into a North Country family of minor gentry, connected across the generations by a heritage of public duty and Liberal politics. Fashionably attractive, she had pale skin, very dark hair, an elegantly long nose (the sign of good breeding) and velvety eyes. Her engaging personality was not dulled by too much education; apart from a couple of years at a Newcastle boarding school, she was educated at home and furnished with the traditional feminine accomplishments of watercolour painting and piano playing, at both of which she excelled. She loved amateur dramatics, animals, her family and God – not necessarily in that order.

So far, so conventional: a pleasant future beckoned, to be spent in sunny morning rooms, visiting the local poor, tucking up the children in their nursery and hosting her husband's guests at dinner. She would grow up to be a good woman, a charitable and pure-minded influence on her friends and family. Hers would be a life well lived.

It *was* a life well lived, but not at all as one would imagine. One of the few purely personal memories in Josephine's published reminiscences hints at what was to come. It is a winter day in Northumberland. The hilly landscape is austere, streaked with waterfalls and rocky underfoot. Two riders emerge from the mist at a gallop, heads pressed low to their horses' manes to avoid the cutting hail. Their clothes have frozen to their bodies, soaked by sweat and the weather, so that when they reach home, they have to peel them off, cheeks glowing. They laugh, exhausted and exhilarated.

These are not rough country lads, but young ladies. Their names are Hatty and Josey Grey, famous locally for their fearlessness, brains and beauty. Hatty wants to run away to the circus when she grows up; her elder sister Josey might join her, as long as she is allowed to bring along her piano and Newfoundland dog. To modern eyes, the pair might appear like unlikely characters from a clichéd romantic novel, fictional escapees from *Wuthering Heights* (but more cheerful). Yet Josephine's idiosyncrasy was real. The suffragist Maude Royden once described her as 'designed by nature for happiness'.[1] Life might have been blissfully easy for her, despite her love of adventure, had she only behaved as she should.

Later, Josephine was to be reviled as disgusting – a criminal, immoral, a procuress; she was damned in Parliament and denounced by the press. Some contemporary commentators considered her literally the devil in disguise; yet others worshipped her as a patron saint of women, 'one of the great people of the world'.[2] She was an iconoclast, a complex individual in a changing world, and about as far from a stereotype as one can imagine.

*

Josephine's father, landowner John Grey (1785–1868), was a respected agricultural reformer, a committed abolitionist and something of a political philosopher. He inherited his family's tendency to activism, campaigning for free trade and the repeal of the Corn Laws, and tax exemptions for his tenants. Daughter Josey continued the tradition. The women of her family were similarly outspoken. Her mother Hannah (*née* Annett, 1794–1860) was of Huguenot silk-weaving stock, brought up in the Moravian tradition, which stresses the importance of a personal relationship with Jesus Christ.

Josephine's paternal aunt Margaretta Grey is said to have once disguised herself as a man in order to penetrate the strangers' gallery at the House of Commons (where women were forbidden) because she was interested in the day's debate and did not see why she should not be there. Aunt

Margaretta was a staunch believer in educating women to lead useful lives, deploring the current fashion of hothousing them as decorative objects who could – and frequently did – bore themselves to death. It is tempting to ascribe Josephine's idealism to her father, her spirituality to her mother and her pragmatism to Aunt Margaretta. Josephine was supremely pragmatic, and in an age when strong female role models were hard to come by, Margaretta was good value.

John and Hannah Grey had ten children, only one of whom died in infancy. Josephine was the seventh. The family moved from their small country estate in the north Cheviot village of Milfield, where Josephine was born, to a substantial house in Dilston, near Corbridge, in 1835. It was designed for John Grey on his appointment as manager of Greenwich Hospital's extensive interests in the area, including farms, lead mines and collieries.

Even though she received scant formal education, Josephine was remarkably well informed. The family freely discussed politics and the principles of liberty and natural justice. At Dilston, the door was always open, with constant visitors arriving from Britain and abroad to discuss the practice and philosophy of agriculture with John. Josephine often accompanied him on his rounds of the Greenwich estate and enjoyed learning about the tenants' lives. Once a year, Hexham Workhouse sent its resident children to Dilston for a party, when John Grey used to dance with them. He was a kindly man and extremely close to Josey.

Her siblings used to say that Josephine was the prettiest and sweetest-tempered of them all. 'I wish I could send her over to you to look at for a while,' wrote one of her sisters to another. 'Everybody loves her so much, nearly everybody thinks she is the nicest girl in the world, next to their own wife or daughter, so you know she must be the *nicest*, as the aforesaid wives and daughters are only nicest to their own husbands and fathers.'[3]

Nice she may have been; complacent she was not. Intensely intelligent and conscientious sometimes to the point of disability, Josephine was troubled all her life by sporadic feelings of spiritual inadequacy. In her late teens, she negotiated a mental crisis, unable to reconcile the ineluctable evils of the world – slavery, poverty, sickness and misfortune – with the concept of God as love. She remembered spending hours in the woods around Dilston shrieking at God to explain Himself. Too shy to voice her doubts to her parents, or to the local vicar, she began a first-hand conversation with God that was to last until death, sustaining and challenging her in equal measure.

Josephine was in her early twenties when she met George Butler (1819-1890), a classics tutor at Durham University. He was eligible: the eldest of the Dean of Peterborough's ten children, educated at Harrow, gifted academically and an energetic sportsman, huntsman, fisherman and shot. Possibly more attractive to Josephine than all these were his obvious humility and an unexpected sense of mischief, demonstrated by his unerring ability to knock chimney pots off their stacks with a single stone. It still took six months of poems and protestations of love to win his 'rose of Dilstone [sic]'.

> Its beauty glads the passer-by
> Its fragrance fills the vale of Tyne;
> No other rose, no flower would I
> Were but the Rose of Dilstone mine.[4]

When he proposed in January 1851, Josephine fretted about his age (he was a decade older than she) and the fact that they had not spent much time in each other's company. And those poems . . .

Records of their courtship are sparse; once George had assured her that he believed marriage to be a perfect and equal partnership of freedom and proved to her that despite the poetry and love letters, he was 'not the *least* spooney',[5] she succumbed. They married at St Andrew's Church, Corbridge, on 8 January 1852.

The Butlers settled in Oxford when George was appointed a public examiner both for the university and for the East India Company's civil service. For years, he had resisted his father's wish that he take Holy Orders. 'You know that I don't like parsons,' he complained to Josephine.[6] This was less to do with theology than an aversion to dressing up in fancy outfits and intoning things in a silly clerical voice. But in 1854, he capitulated, realising that ordination was a sensible next step in his career. At the time, many of the university's professors were also Anglican clergymen, and George hoped for a Chair in Classics. Neither Josephine nor George considered his ordination to be in any way cynical, despite his reservations about performing in church. At the core of their Christian faith was the conviction that a personal relationship with God superseded ritual. Spiritual integrity was paramount. Josephine admired her husband for achieving this in the face of the Anglican congregation's occasional foibles – and his own.

The couple lived in a series of rented rooms in Oxford. George's hours during term were not onerous, with the corollary that his salary was low. (During the vacations he fulfilled his East India Company duties in London, while Josephine returned to Dilston.) Always intellectually curious, Josephine worked with him on various moneymaking ventures: editing an unexpurgated edition of Chaucer, for which – unusually for a female – she was allowed access to the university's Bodleian library, and collating a catalogue of

Renaissance drawings in Oxford. For leisure, she painted in watercolours, played her piano and rode on horseback with George to nearby Bagley Woods to listen to the nightingales.

She used to dress in white silk and lace to perform when George's colleagues and academic friends came round of an evening, proudly noting that no one so much as coughed during her recitals, so transfixed were they by the music and, no doubt, by this amiable young woman with the raven hair and expressive eyes. Given her liberal, fresh-air upbringing, she was shocked by their reaction to her attempts to join the conversation after dinner. Offering them a flawless Beethoven sonata was fine. Expressing a personal opinion, while expecting to be taken seriously, was not. Usually she kept quiet, to avoid embarrassing George. But sometimes she could not.

In 1853, Elizabeth Gaskell's novel *Ruth* was published. It was condemned by many as immoral, verging on the obscene, for suggesting that its protagonist – a young, unmarried mother – was not the author of her own downfall. The Oxford academics sitting around the Butlers' drawing room fire harrumphed at Mrs Gaskell's wrongheadedness, insisting that it was far safer for society that women be kept institutionally naïve. Ignorance is bliss. Everyone had tales to tell of promising undergraduates and tutors (who were all male and mostly unmarried at that time) being traduced by loose women into fatherhood. One such involved a 'child-mother'[7] who had recently been imprisoned for infanticide, after the man who got her in the family way refused to acknowledge her or his baby. No action was taken against *him*, naturally; *she* was sent to Newgate gaol.

Josephine was appalled. This sort of prejudice smacked of the injustices of slavery her father used to tell her about; it was an abuse of power and a denial of human rights. 'Every instinct of womanhood within me was in revolt,' she remembered later.

The only reason for women being on earth at all, she decided, was to be combatants against 'certain accepted theories in society'.[8] She was ready for the fight.

*

With George's support, Josephine marched off to tackle theologian Benjamin Jowett, arguably the most influential Oxford academic of his generation. Perhaps he did not realize the implication of this moral double standard? Though admiring of female intellect, which was uncommon for a man in his position, and generally regarded by the university as something of a sage, Jowett rejected her argument that disadvantaged women were victimized by a patriarchal society (though she did not, of course, use those words). 'She is very excitable and emotional, of an over-sympathetic temperament,' he wrote to his unemotional friend and confidante, Florence Nightingale. This leads her to take an interest, he continued, in 'a class of sinners whom she had better have left to themselves.' He warned Josephine that her agitation could only do harm. 'It is dangerous to arouse a sleeping lion.'[9]

Josephine ignored him. She said of her husband that 'the idea of justice to women, of equality between the sexes, and of equality of responsibility of all human beings top the moral law, seems to have been instinctive in him.'[10] In this they were perfectly matched. To Josephine, loving one's neighbour as oneself was a moral imperative. It informed everything she did. Together, she and George contacted the chaplain at Newgate, identified the convicted woman, and offered her sanctuary.

Though never named by the Butlers, on her release this young outcast joined their growing family as a housemaid. Josephine could not have been prouder of her husband for helping to put their beliefs into practice, in spite of the effect such wild behaviour was bound to have on his prospects. 'I think [the Newgate girl] was the first of a world of unhappy women he welcomed into his own home,' noted Josephine. 'She was not the last.'[11]

The Butlers' first child, George Grey (Georgie), was born in November 1852. Josephine refused attendance by a doctor, as she did for all her confinements. She tended not to trust them (though later she consulted the female medical pioneer Dr Agnes McLaren). Her health had never been robust, despite a childhood led largely out of doors, and she suffered recurrent and often non-specific problems with both heart and lungs. Giving birth seems to have left her unusually debilitated, but Arthur Stanley (known by his second name) arrived safely in 1854, and a third son, Charlie, two years later.

Despite a house – or set of rooms – full of children under five years old, Josephine felt restless and underemployed. She walked the unsavoury streets of Oxford at night, during a local cholera epidemic, looking for women she might help as she had helped the Newgate girl. This was before the widespread organization of agencies dedicated to so-called 'rescue work' among prostitutes. It is likely, therefore, that all Josephine could do is talk to them, hold their hands, occasionally give them small bunches of flowers to make them feel human again.

Three things were necessary, she felt, for her to continue this welfare work while preserving her sanity. One was God's approval. Another was her family's support – both her husband's, and her parents' and siblings'; the last was a sense of proportion. This understandably deserted her at times, but humour helped. In Oxford she was tickled when one of the prostitutes she met turned out to be a circus-girl, just like she and Hatty once longed to be. Her 'acrobatic performances were the most innocent part of her role,'[12] noted Josephine archly. Thank goodness the sisters had given up their ambition to ride standing up in the saddle for a living and had married good men instead. Hatty had by now become the wife of a Swiss banker and lived in Naples; you couldn't get much better than that.

The Oxford circus-girl was invited to join the increasingly colourful Butler household, while George's baffled colleagues considered how to react to his bizarre behaviour. Were the Revd. George and his wife bad or mad? His career stalled; the professorship he had been hoping for failed to materialize. Josephine's health began to deteriorate (trouble with the lungs again, exacerbated by the city's notoriously damp atmosphere). They were running out of room, and might soon run out of friends. It was time to move on.

In 1857, George Butler was offered the post of vice principal at Cheltenham College, a boys' school in the famously salubrious spa town. His salary increased, and the family was installed in a large Regency house shared by a number of pupil boarders. A year later, Josephine fell pregnant again. Evangeline Mary, her 'angel' Eva, was born in April 1859.

Despite her indifferent health, the next five years passed relatively serenely for Josephine. In 1861, she and nine-year-old Georgie made a voyage from Folkestone to Boulogne and kept a comic diary between them, full of in-jokes and affection. A friend sharing a Lake District summer holiday with the Butlers recalled evenings when Josephine was surrounded by her laughing children, talking in low voices like lovers. They would all romp around during the day and then swim in the moonlight.

Maude Royden was right: this woman was designed for happiness. So why choose, a few years later, to walk – as another friend put it – straight into the jaws of hell?

2

Campaigns and crusades

It took Josephine 30 years to write about the death of her daughter Eva. It was brutally unexpected. On the afternoon of Saturday, 20 August 1864, the family had just returned from one of their summer holidays in the Lake District, and everyone was busy. When Josephine was asked by Eva for a little box to house a rescued caterpillar, she found her something and then told her to trot away and play. That was the last time they spoke.

Exactly what happened that evening is unclear; though she remembered the immediate aftermath of the accident, Josephine could never bring herself to articulate the details. The entrance hall of their Cheltenham home had a stone floor and a sweeping staircase, with a galleried landing above. Eva must have been up in the nursery when she impulsively decided to rush down for a hug from her parents before dinner. Either she ran to the balustrade and overbalanced, or she toppled from the banisters while sliding down them (as all the children loved to do).

There was a suggestion that the butler, who was in the hall below, might have caught her had he moved quickly enough, but he had taken cover, thinking Eva's brothers were playing their habitual game of cushion-throwing. The governess shrieked as Eva fell. George picked up the child and a doctor was immediately sent for, but Eva died soon afterwards. 'Never can I lose that memory,' wrote Josephine later. 'The fall, the sudden cry, and then the silence . . . Would to God that I had died that death for her.'[1]

The family was shattered. Two years afterwards, they left Cheltenham for northwest England on George's appointment as headmaster of Liverpool College. At first the move was unhelpful to Josephine, who sat alone all day while the boys were at school and pined for her golden-haired daughter. Her physical and mental health declined, and for the second time in her life she suffered a crisis of faith she feared might overwhelm her. Conversation with God became more urgent than ever. 'I long to have a hundred voices, that with all of them I might pray without ceasing that Christ will come quickly, and deliver forever the poor groaning world.'[2] No one, she imagined, groaned with more sorrow than she.

Two things saved Josephine from complete despair. Her upbringing had taught her that sorrow should not be a vehicle for self-pity, but compassion. And she had the emotional intelligence to realize that though happiness was out of her hands, at least she need not be lonely. George and the boys found solace in activity; she tried to do the same. 'I became possessed with an irresistible desire to go forth and find some pain keener than my own – to meet with people more unhappy than myself . . . My sole wish was to plunge into the heart of some human misery and to say (as I now knew I could) to afflicted people, "I understand. I, too, have suffered."'[3]

*

After her experiences in Oxford, Josephine knew just where to find the afflicted people she sought. She had only to step onto the streets of Liverpool and look into the eyes of the fallen women she found at almost every corner. Not far from the Butler home was Brownlow Hill workhouse, the biggest such institution in the country, with a shifting population of up to 5000 destitute people. (Its vast complex of buildings was demolished in the 1930s; Liverpool's Catholic Cathedral occupies the site now.) As well as segregated dormitories and refectories, it included an infirmary and its own Bridewell, or reformatory, where women convicted of public nuisance offences were 'corrected'. Most of them were common prostitutes.

The term 'common prostitute' was coined in the Vagrancy Act of 1824, which criminalized those who lived off immoral earnings. Indigent women were penalized long before that, however, by a succession of Poor Law Acts dating from the sixteenth century, referring to them as evil, lewd and vicious. Prostitution *per se* was not illegal, but various transgressions associated with it were; soliciting, for example, or pimping. Illegitimacy became a synonym for sinfulness by association, when the easy connection was made between prostitution and the bearing of bastard children. Indeed, any woman known to have had sex outside marriage was popularly presumed guilty of a legal as well as a moral misdemeanour, and liable to punishment. Any man known to have had sex outside marriage was popularly presumed to be sowing his wild oats.

The women visited by Josephine at Brownlow Hill were outcasts: emblems of society's corruption pushed out of sight and out of mind. It is true, however, that by now – this was 1866 – attitudes to the 'fallen' were beginning to change. Mrs Gaskell was not the only popular author to write about such people with sympathy. Think of Charles Dickens's *Oliver Twist*, George Eliot's *Silas Marner*, Anthony Trollope's

Doctor Thorne. A growing number of Christian rescue homes opened in British towns and cities, and though it is not always clear what was being rescued by getting her off the streets – the 'sinner' or the society she threatened – there were occasional attempts at rehabilitation. Pioneers like Felicia Skene and Ellice Hopkins worked to prevent the causes of economic and spiritual poverty and so make society a healthier and holier place for everyone. (Miss Hopkins memorably suggested that a fence at the top of a precipice was better than an ambulance at the foot, neatly encapsulating the concept of preventative public health.[4])

For all her libertarian ideals, Josephine Butler considered prostitutes, whom she insisted on calling 'women of the city', to be sinners. What set her apart was her refusal to condemn them for it and her insistence that men who bought sex were at least as culpable as women who sold it. She also maintained that sinfulness was not endemic; it could be cured. 'Courage, my darlings,' she would say to the most degraded of her new friends. 'You are women, and a woman is always a beautiful thing.'[5]

Was she naïve? In denial? It is easy for us to perceive Victorian poverty through a sanitizing haze of sentimentality; that is, after all, how most contemporary illustrators presented it. The deserving poor were like earthbound angels, inwardly pure and really rather lovely, as long as you could not smell them or count the crawling lice in their hair. Did Josephine feel the same way, using a carefully managed relationship with them as a prop to make her feel less wretched? In reality, these 'beautiful things' were probably filthy, hungry, foul-mouthed and defensive. If we believe that Josephine appreciated this, her positivity on their behalf is astounding.

The evidence is in her favour. She did not claim to be a proselytizer, a collector of converts or saviour of souls. She was an evangelist who believed in the power of forgiveness. It was her mission to convince the women amongst whom she worked that they deserved forgiveness, no matter how deeply they had been dragged – or had dragged themselves – into the mire. This could only be done through kindness and a recognition not of their outward state but their essential human dignity. And she was enough of an iconoclast to enjoy the thought of pompous do-gooders 'startled by seeing the poor lost dregs of humanity dancing into heaven before them.'[6] She never had time for hypocrites; neither the hypocrites who condemned women for prostitution while using prostitutes themselves, nor those who claimed to be Christians while doing their best to close the pearly gates to all but a select few.

It was no surprise to George Butler that his wife chose the inmates of Brownlow Hill for her companions. Though still distraught by Eva's death and grappling with the demands of a new job, he supported Josephine's social idiosyncrasy. A headmaster's wife should surely find enough occupation in entertaining his colleagues and influential parents. Josephine was too busy consorting with whores. She was allowed into the Bridewell's oakum sheds, where inmates earned their keep (an interesting concept for a prison) by picking apart old rope, strand by strand, to be used for caulking ships. It left the hands raw and stinking. When elegant Mrs Butler squatted down among them and tried to untangle the fibres herself, she was so inept, and the whole thing so unlikely, that her companions laughed. She laughed with them.

This is where Josephine's fight began, against the moral and practical injustices of a society terrified by weakness and riven by double standards. Always within a Christian framework – but not judgementally – she introduced hopeless women to the concept of redemption. She told them Bible stories of unconditional love; prayed gently with them; introduced them to her home and family; even took them in and personally cared for them, as she had the child-murderess and the circus-girl in Oxford.

*

Josephine's copious writings are full of unlikely heroines who influenced her. The first of them was Mary Lomax. Mary's was an old, old story: she was raped by a gentleman of the house while working in service, thrown out by her respectable parents, inveigled into a brothel in Liverpool with nowhere else to go and then thrown out again when she developed tuberculosis. She attempted suicide in the workhouse, survived, though seriously consumptive by now, and met Josephine in the oakum sheds when she was 24.

Josephine took Mary home on her release. For the last three months of her life she was part of a loving family. She converted to Christianity under George's direction and, according to Josephine, died happy. Perhaps this long and strangely positive goodbye was therapeutic for Josephine, given the suddenness of Eva's death. Her grief for Mary was more comfortable than eviscerating; she bought expensive white camellias (which she could not afford) to line the coffin and laid the young woman to rest beside her sister Hatty's daughter, who had died two years after Eva.

When the Butlers' bedrooms, cellars and attics became full, Josephine rented what she called a 'House of Rest' for women hoping to reform but with nowhere to go but back to the streets or the brothel. As a next step, she set up a 'factory' where they were paid for such menial and inoffensive tasks as folding envelopes or taking in laundry. The money to run

both establishments came from her – and therefore George's
– own pockets, with limited financial support from certain
Liverpool doctors who recognized the economic and moral
benefits of erasing prostitution, even if only one person at a
time, and from North Country activists who, like Josephine,
worked for the status of women to be raised across society.

It was arguably during the 1860s that British women woke
up to the power of solidarity. Josephine credited her firebrand
ancestors with her own appetite for activism. Before the
campaign against the Contagious Diseases Acts consumed
her in 1869, she had a finger in several radical pies. In 1866,
the year the family moved to Liverpool, she signed John
Stuart Mill's famous petition to Parliament in favour of votes
for women. She was passionate about the potential of good
women to improve society, but in order to do so, they needed
a meaningful voice. She later learned to influence politics
through protest, but at this stage in her reforming career, she
was still an idealist.

She remained a suffragist all her life; it was the slowest-
moving of all her causes: universal suffrage was not achieved
until the centenary of her birth, in 1928. It was also the most
fundamental. Without political power, women's opinions
were negligible; only a vote could confer that power. But one
campaign led to another. This was first-wave feminism in all
its glory: a spreading awareness of the importance of shared
purpose and mutual support.

For example: if women were to have a vote, they required
access to the sort of education that would empower them to use it
responsibly. In 1867, both George and Josephine were involved
in setting up the North of England Council for Promoting
the Higher Education of Women. Their co-founder was a
Liverpudlian teacher, Anne Jemima Clough, the sister of one

of George's oldest friends. Josephine served as secretary to the Council from its inception until 1873, spearheading petitions demanding rigorous public examinations for schoolgirls (established as 'Cambridge Higher Locals' in 1869) and opportunities for successful candidates to study at Cambridge University (resulting in the foundation of Girton and Newnham Colleges in 1869 and 1871, respectively).

But that was not enough. If female undergraduates were to get the most out of their university education, they must have high-calibre teachers. Hence the Butlers' enthusiasm for what was called the University Extension scheme: series of lectures given by respected academics or enthusiasts on subjects ranging from astronomy to zoology. They were delivered specifically to groups of women at various locations around the country. Or to groups of ladies: few working-class wives and daughters would have the time or money to spend on learning.

And so the *next* campaign was born: what was a female to do once she graduated? Skip home with her trophy, sit tight and wait for her wedding (while painfully aware that gentlemen do not generally marry bluestockings)? In 1868, Josephine's first book was published, *The Education and Employment of Women*. An edition of essays, *Woman's Work and Woman's Culture*, followed in 1869. Both works imply that women's economic dependence on their fathers and then their husbands stymies their intellectual development and moral dignity, and that sexual equality in the home and the workplace lifts us all that much closer to happiness and to God.

Talking of sexual equality: in 1868, Josephine joined the Married Women's Property Committee. This was a pressure group lobbying for the right of a wife to possess her own wealth. Before the Married Women's Property Act was passed in 1882 (whereupon the Committee was dissolved), virtually everything a wife possessed was passed to her husband on and during marriage: inheritance, salary (if she were radical enough to earn one), rent and property. To Josephine, steeped as she was in the tenets of abolitionism, this smacked of domestic slavery. Besides, any piece of legislation acknowledging women to be separate entities, belonging to themselves rather than to some man, was to be welcomed. Had women the vote, no such pressure group would be necessary – which brings us back round to the suffrage campaign, where we began.

The same people tend to surface in any discussion of women's activism during the late nineteenth century, many of them based around Liverpool and Manchester. The autodidact and endlessly energetic Lydia Becker is one; proto-feminist Elizabeth Wolstenholme another, with Anne Jemima Clough and Millicent Fawcett. According to Josephine, these women were 'some of the nicest and most real people I ever met'.[7] She was proud to be associated with them, and it was gratifying to feel oneself at the vanguard of change, even if that change came painfully slowly.

Victory was not the only criterion for success, however. The network created by these interrelated campaigns for women's rights gave those involved a sense of agency – a novel experience for women reformers in Britain – and an opportunity to practise the unfamiliar routines of committee meetings, public speaking and legal procedure. Josephine could not have had a better platform from which to launch the one crusade which above all others was to define her life's work: the repeal of the Contagious Diseases Acts.[8]

*

The letter of the law might have changed over the centuries, but the spirit of the Contagious Diseases Acts (CDAs) of 1864-1869 was nothing new. When Henry VIII fretted about the below-par performance of his fighting forces, he blamed prostitutes for wilfully spreading syphilis, corrupting his soldiers both physically and morally. Before then, organized prostitution was tolerated, with certain exclusions and regulations, but after a Royal Proclamation of 1546, it was nominally outlawed – to very little effect.

Early in 1864, a Bill to address the spread of 'cattle plague' was debated in Parliament. A few months later, in the drowsy depths of summer, a piece of legislation called the Contagious Diseases Act received royal assent. It was generally assumed by the few people who noticed it that this must be something to do with cattle too. But a different creature was specified in the small print: it was all about women. Its provisions were harsh. In an attempt to contain rampant levels of venereal disease (VD) in the British forces, any woman believed to be a prostitute operating in 11 specified army camps and naval bases could be forcibly apprehended, registered, internally examined and if found to be diseased, incarcerated for up to three months in a 'lock hospital' until healed by treatment with mercury, or time.

The 1864 Act was experimental; two years later another CDA was passed, adding more locations and compulsory fortnightly examinations of suspected women. The third and final CDA was passed in the summer of 1869, extending the reach of the authorities even further and lengthening the period of possible detention to nine months.

Plainclothes police were drafted in to the targeted towns to hunt for prey, with the result that perfectly respectable wives and daughters unable to afford a carriage to get home were vulnerable to arrest. They had no right to appeal to a trial by jury. The invasive examinations they were forced to undergo were painful, dangerous (efficiently spreading disease through repeated use of unsterilized instruments) and akin to what protesters called 'steel rape'. The police could be indiscriminate, seizing any woman available to fulfil their arrest quotas. The stigma of subjection to this process was ineradicable, since no proper distinction was made between the innocent and the guilty.

These measures might have had a better chance of achieving their disinfectant role had men been targeted as well as women, issued with condoms, allowed to marry whatever their rank or taught to think of every female they met as their mother or a sister (all suggestions made at the time), but none of those solutions addressed the implicit inequity of the CDAs. To those who supported them, they promised to limit VD, reduce the distasteful incidence of diseased men polluting their 'clean' wives, save money on medical treatment and make sure Britain won the next war. To those opposed to the Acts – like Josephine and George Butler – they condoned the state regulation of vice, creating a class of certified sex slaves. They objectified women, constitutionally exempting them from their human rights and presenting them as vessels to be used, cleaned out, and used again until fit for nothing but the grave.

Something must be done.

3

Revolt of the women

'[T]wo words from the mouth of a woman, speaking in the name of all women. And these two words are – we rebel!'[1] Josephine made this call to arms at a conference of CDA protesters in May 1870. She had spent the previous summer in Switzerland with members of the family, trying to recover her perennially precarious health while canvassing wider support for the women's education campaign. On her return, she was appalled to learn of the passing of the third CDA from friends' messages waiting for her at Dover harbour. Among them was a telegram from a doctor in Nottingham, Charles Worth, who knew of and admired Josephine's work with prostitutes in Liverpool. Its message was urgent: 'Haste to the rescue!'

She did – but not straight away. The National Association for the Repeal of the Contagious Diseases Acts (NA) was formed after a meeting of concerned activists in Bristol in September 1869; bizarrely, women were excluded from membership. Or perhaps not so bizarrely: institutional naivety was rife, and it was thought dangerous to female sensibilities to subject them to the sort of shocking revelations involved in any discussion of the CDAs. This attitude harked back to the early days of Queen Victoria's reign, when a prototype of the CDAs was discussed – following the state regulation of vice by Napoleon in France – but then abandoned by politicians said to have baulked at the idea of laying such an embarrassing piece of legislation before an innocent young lady for signing off.

A Ladies' National Association (LNA) was formed soon afterwards by Elizabeth Wolstenholme, with the stellar support of Florence Nightingale, Harriet Martineau and a caucus of staunchly unshockable activists from around the country. Between October and December, Josephine agonized over what she increasingly came to regard as a call from God to lead them, the vocation for which she had been preparing all her life. This mission to repeal the CDAs would be difficult enough to accept, given its abhorrent nature, had she only herself to consider. What about George and the children?

It took time to find the courage to tell her husband about the call. In fact she wrote him a letter instead, quietly delivering it to him in his study. A few days' strained silence followed, before he turned to her and simply said 'Go! And the Lord be with you.'[2]

Josephine was immediately appointed secretary of the LNA, which was run from the crowded Butler household in Liverpool. She was an obvious choice as figurehead and chief spokeswoman, being highly politically aware, conscientious and hardworking, as well as charismatic, easy on the eye and passionate, but never strident, with a heritage of radical activism. A 'Ladies' Appeal and Protest' was published in *The Daily News* on 1 January 1870, outlining opposition to the CDAs and signed by 124 LNA members. Energetic, influential gentlemen were rallied to the cause, among them Professor James Stuart, a colleague from University Extension days who became a close family friend; a steel manufacturer from Sheffield, Henry Wilson, whose wife Charlotte was a member of the LNA; and Liberal MP Sir James Stansfeld. Literature was published, letters written, petitions signed (one of which included over 250,000 signatures and was a staggering five miles long) and a punishing series of public lectures launched.

Josephine's first speaking engagement was at Crewe, where she opened a short tour of northern towns to a sympathetic audience of railway workers. As the years went by, she became an extremely accomplished orator, swiftly finding fame as the slender, sweet-voiced, fashionably dressed and graceful lady from whose mouth issued the most devastating indecencies. She spoke of the iniquity of treating women as 'ticketed human flesh'[3] (CDA inspectors issued them with dockets to prove they were clean) and of comforting them after botched examinations as they lay weeping, lips white, hands blue and petticoats drenched with blood. She accused supporters of the CDAs of oppression, blasphemy and moral bankruptcy, and blamed the whole of society for driving women 'as sheep to the slaughter into the slave markets of London.'[4] She repeated to public audiences what had been told to her in the privacy of the prison cell or lock-hospital ward, like this heartfelt cry from a prostitute she met in Chatham, Kent.

> To please a man I did wrong at first, then I was flung about from man to man, men police lay hands on us. By men we are examined, handled, doctored and messed on with. In the hospital, it is a man again makes prayers and reads the Bible for us. We are had up before magistrates who are men, and we never get out of the hands of men till we die.[5]

Hundreds of women came to Josephine's meetings, as well as men. The press started to take notice, with opinion divided according to editors' predilections. Mrs Butler was a saint, an angel, a female Christ, the champion of the working class and the bravest woman on earth. Or a public danger, a vulgar showgirl, an 'indecent Maenad' (or madwoman), a narcissist of the highest order. She was a celebrity, notorious, subjected to a peculiarly Victorian brand of weirdness in the comments of those who only went to hear her out of curiosity, commenting on the unusual length of her nose, her penchant for fur tippets, her intriguing appetite for salacious debate. The poet John Adington Symonds was interested to note that his 'sexual equipment swelled'[6] at the sound of her voice: there was obviously a vicarious thrill to be had from the spectacle of a respectable woman discussing degeneracy.

*

Some characters lend themselves to caricature (from now on, I'm including Symonds among them). Florence Nightingale, the lady of the lamp, is popularly portrayed as a compassionate, caring soul who loved her fellow human beings with complete devotion. In fact, she could be coldly clinical, waspish and prone to professional jealousy.[7] Josephine Butler – though less familiar to us now than she was a century ago – is similarly presented as a paragon of selflessness. But she was not perfect.

She was quite capable of insulting those with whom she disagreed, resorting to taunts about their appearance or personality. Strangely for an abolitionist, she was careless about describing people of colour, noting that some of the African pupils at George's school had only half-civilized parents. She once mentioned receiving a letter from what is now Mozambique which looked rather dark and stained by the time it dropped through her letterbox, 'having been carried in the belt of the native, perhaps next his brown skin'.[8] She could be an inverted snob, claiming neither to know nor care about members of the aristocracy or middle classes. 'I found they did not understand my language, nor I theirs.'[9] She was undoubtedly middle class herself – but resented the assumptions made about her for that reason.

Her private notebooks chronicle a troubled conscience over the way she treated her husband and sons. She bitterly regretted her (unspecified) unkindness to them and admitted to being neglectful. Luckily the boys won scholarships to university, as the LNA and Josephine's other causes had sucked up all the Butler money and Josephine's jewellery. Young Charlie, the closest in age and relationship to Eva, was a strangely quiet and melancholy child whom she had no time to comfort fully.

In years to come, the impact of Josephine's work on her children would become more apparent; at this stage, it appears to have been manageable. Charlie helped seal envelopes in the LNA office, and Stanley, aged around 20, conducted some unlikely undercover research while 'accidentally' attending a ball in a Paris brothel where most of the guests, he was surprised to find, were naked. One longs to know more about this escapade, but the archives are frustratingly silent.

George Butler's prospects had looked bright at the start of his career: academic Victorian clergymen with accomplished and beautiful wives could go far. His chances of success diminished in direct proportion to Josephine's growing profile, however. The roll at Liverpool College began to fall. George was shouted down when he spoke in public in the course of clerical or educational duties and was denied preferment, according to Josephine, because he lived in a home with several former prostitutes and an immodest wife. He sacrificed a great deal.

As well as worrying about money, reputation, children and career, poor George was constantly stressed by the level of condemnation faced by his frail-looking wife. This was a reactive age, when political dissent could be expressed directly with boot and fist. Josephine was attacked on several fronts. First in the queue were the politicians, military personnel, medical men and moral vigilantes who designed and upheld the CDAs, some of them eager to extend the Acts' reach to the civilian population. Then came the Victorian equivalents of Mr and Mrs 'Disgusted Tunbridge Wells', outraged by a female elbowing herself onto the public stage and spouting filth. At their backs were women who relied on prostitution to keep themselves and their families, and who regarded the tickets given to them by CDA inspectors after examination as professional qualifications. This was never a straightforward battle between oppressive men and victimized women. Some of Josephine's strongest supporters were men; some of her most rancorous enemies women.

At times the opposition was physical. She was kicked to the ground by medical students in Manchester and needed a 24-man bodyguard in Essex. In October 1870, there was a bye-election in the garrison town of Colchester after the incumbent Liberal MP died. The Liberal government selected Sir Henry Storks as a shoe-in candidate to succeed him, anxious for his expertise in Cabinet as a military administrator. Storks was a CDA man; he had introduced regulation of prostitutes while Governor of Malta. The NA and LNA were determined to block his election by fielding another Liberal candidate sympathetic to their cause, therefore splitting Storks's vote.

Josephine journeyed to Colchester to campaign. She describes a ladies' meeting there in *Personal Reminiscences of a Great Crusade*, the closest account we have to a published autobiography. She was refused admittance at her hotel, because Storks's supporters threatened to burn it down if she stayed there. She was given a grubby shawl and disguised as a poor local woman to get into the venue for the meeting. Afterwards, she was smuggled out and hidden among the bacon and soap in a grocer's shop to avoid the mob. Storks was defeated, much to her satisfaction.

It was heartening, too, that the government opened a Royal Commission on the Administration and Operation of the Contagious Diseases Acts, partly due to the Colchester result. It ran for 45 days from January 1871, calling on scores of medical men, matrons at lock-hospitals, rescue workers, even an undertaker, who was asked how many paupers he had buried last year. The answer was 800. It used to be more – from which the Commissioners inferred that fewer women in poverty were dying of VD and therefore the CDAs were working.

Josephine took the stand in March, stressing the constitutional injustice done to women affected by the CDAs. They were assumed guilty without the means to prove themselves innocent; their treatment was barbaric; the message sent to society by the enactment of this corrupt legislation was universally demeaning, expecting vicious behaviour from half of the population while punishing the other half for accommodating it.

For good measure, Josephine added that the age of consent was too low in Britain (12 years old), which encouraged the vile practice of selling children into sexual slavery. And the Bastardy laws needed reforming, while we're at it, to relieve single women of sole responsibility for their illegitimate children.

The Commissioners' findings were published in a series of mealy-mouthed reports in the summer of 1871, some in favour of repeal or amendment of the CDAs, others advocating their extension. Statistics were flaunted to prove that the Acts were succeeding in lowering the incidence of VD; matching statistics proved the opposite. Some hospital matrons insisted they had never heard an inmate express discomfort while being internally examined; others, including Josephine, said they had witnessed the violent penetration of girls as young as 13 at the hands of 'beasts'. She meant the doctors, earning a living off lust. The initial optimism of Josephine and her allies evaporated while politicians bickered and filibustered over the reports' conclusions, and subsequent attempts to change the status quo came and went.

In August 1872, the action shifted to Pontefract in Yorkshire, where Liberal Hugh Childers was up for re-election. The repealers' campaign here was less about personality – though Childers, as First Lord of the Admiralty, had been responsible for instituting the Acts in Portsmouth and Plymouth – and more about policy. Prime Minister William Gladstone had recently withdrawn a Bill partially to repeal the CDAs; Pontefract would be an opportunity to protest. Josephine was in the thick of things. She explained in a letter to her children (who must have been aghast) what happened when she tried to hold another ladies' meeting. The only venue she could find to host her and Charlotte Wilson, her sister speaker, was a hayloft above a room where bundles of straw were stored. It was reached via a ladder leading through a trap door. When they clambered up, the women found the floor of the loft covered in a thick sprinkling of cayenne pepper, which stained their skirts, caught in their throats and made their eyes water. Josephine was struggling to speak through the pepper fumes when there was a smell of burning, and smoke began to curl up through the floorboards. The straw below had been set alight, and now angry men were making their way up the ladder to block the women's escape. 'The language was hideous. They shook their fists in our faces, with volleys of oaths.'[10]

Thanks to a young Yorkshire woman in the audience who managed to slip past the marauders and fetch help, the fire was extinguished. But a 'fierce argument' ensued involving stones and broken glass, and without God's intervention, Josephine was convinced that she and Charlotte might well have perished – especially when the two policemen called to the scene did nothing but pop their heads in and then leave 'with a cynical smile'.[11] Eventually the women were released to scuttle away to safety. The Liberal majority was cut by 150 votes at Pontefract, and one third of the 2000 registered voters there abstained: a victory of sorts for the repealers, but better was to come.

*

Adventures like these left Josephine exhausted. All meetings were tiring: after performing on stage, she would often finish too late to catch anything but the mail train home, travelling third class for lack of funds. Frequent bouts of respiratory illness, neuralgia and depression were countered by trips abroad – crowdfunded by friends – and (paradoxically) yet more relentless activity.

In 1874, she engineered the spread of the repeal campaign to Europe, trudging to cities in France and Italy to meet supporters and protesters. Paris was her first stop, where a well-entrenched system of state-regulated vice had been in place for decades, operated by men whose vested interests in the sex industry made them intransigent and hostile. But Josephine was not to be cowed.

She visited a prison for convicted, diseased prostitutes in St Lazare, which she found too disgusting to describe. She met Charles Lecour, Chief of the *Police des Moeurs*, or moral police, responsible for delivering the French equivalent of the CDAs. She considered him vain and pompous, an agent of evil 'intoxicated with the sense of power, chattering and gesticulating like an ape'.[12]

The next few years passed in a shifting haze of fatigue. Sometimes Josephine felt she could clearly see victory on the horizon, before the mist came down again and blotted out any hope of progress. God listened to her, she was sure, but He did not make things easy. She turned 50 in April 1878, as busy as she had ever been with LNA meetings at home and abroad, administration, political lobbying and tending to her 'guests' in Liverpool.

William Gladstone's Liberal party had been defeated in the general election four years previously, when Benjamin Disraeli succeeded him as prime minister. In 1880, Gladstone returned for a second term, rejuvenating the repeal campaign. Research by the LNA and other agencies during the intervening years had uncovered a thriving black economy based on the trafficking of British girls to brothels on the Continent. The work of Josephine and her allies appeared to be fuelling an appetite, at last, for a more wholesome and compassionate approach to the complex problems of the sex industry.

In 1882, Josephine's friend Sir James Stansfeld introduced a Bill to repeal the compulsory examination of women under the Acts, which was stalled while a Select Committee investigated their operation once again. Josephine sat in the Ladies' Gallery at the House of Commons when the legislation was finally debated on 20 April 1883. The division was not called until after midnight; the results of the vote came through just before 1 a.m. The repealers had won.

Right at the beginning of this campaign, members of Parliament confessed to being a little bewildered by protesters in petticoats. 'We know how to manage any other opposition in the House or in the country,' said one of them, 'but this is very awkward for us – this revolt of the women. It is quite a new thing; what are we to do with such an opposition as this?'[13] Ignore it, deny it, shout it down – and, finally, take notice. People cried as they crowded into Westminster Hall after the session ended. Even Stansfeld had tears coursing down his cheeks as he grasped Josephine's hands in wordless triumph.

Josephine herself, though inexpressibly relieved, was dry-eyed. She was an emotional person, even sentimental at times, but her pragmatism was overwhelming. Crying was a particularly useless way of expending precious energy. 'I long ago rejected the old ideal of the "division of labour", that "men must work and women must weep,"'[14] Despite this day of days, she still had a great deal of work to do. And she was growing old and tired: there was no time to waste.

4

Hard work, but God is good

The CDAs were not officially repealed until 1886, but Stansfeld's Bill meant that the legislation was effectively moribund after 1883. That battle was won. Meanwhile, another was brewing, even more lurid than the last. And yet again, Josephine was up there, marching with the Generals.

In 1879, a Quaker publisher called Alfred Dyer travelled to Brussels to investigate rumours of British women being exported to Belgian brothels against their will. The city was notorious to anti-vice campaigners as a modern Babylon where the sex industry was operated by a state cartel, a network of influential men bound together by vested interests and avarice. The local Chief of Police cheerfully admitted that the more brothels there were in his jurisdiction, the merrier, as 'men, for whom houses of debauchery are a necessity, seldom care to take long journeys to find them.'[1]

Dyer knew that the most coveted prostitutes in Brussels were young British girls. Childishness and innocence were at a premium. In Belgium, the age of consent was inconveniently high (21), which meant local supply could not satisfy demand. It was only 13 in Britain (raised from 12 in 1875), so why not source the goods there and sail them across the channel? In practice, this meant kidnapping girls, buying them from their parents, or inveigling them abroad, then keeping them prisoner until no longer profitable.

In the book, he gave examples of people wooed in London under false pretences, lured to Brussels by the promise of marriage, then trapped; others were drugged and stolen from their families, or tricked by well-dressed women into believing there was a glamorous but respectable job waiting for them abroad. He met some of them on his mortifying undercover visits to brothels. They implored him to help them escape – which in some cases, he and his associates were able to do.

Naturally, Dyer was familiar with Josephine's work. He was anxious to enlist her support for his new society, the London Committee for Supporting the Traffic in British Girls, set up in 1880. She was well aware of the situation he described, having made her point about the age of consent to the Royal Commission on the CDAs back in 1871. The fact that it was so low made a travesty of childhood.

Josephine had also been to Brussels – as she had to many major cities in France, Belgium, Switzerland and Italy by now – while campaigning against the CDAs. She was able to add a few weapons to Dyer's arsenal. She claimed that the reason the Chief of Police was so keen on increasing the number of brothels was not really to make prostitution more convenient for men. It was because his own son had been appointed sole supplier of wine to them all. What is more, his second-in-command owned a number of brothels himself: they made money.

Josephine published her findings, with further allegations of police collusion in child trafficking, fully realizing she was vulnerable to a charge of libel. As a retaliatory step, the Belgian police wrote to the Home Office requiring her to repeat her charges under oath – which she did, before a Liverpool magistrate. It was crucial that every statement

The house at Milfield, Northumberland, where Josephine was born. It was demolished in the 1960s. (© Claire Grey)

This marble bust, sculpted by the Butlers' friend Alexander Munro in 1855, presents Josephine as the epitome of femininity. (Northumberland Archives)

Josephine's husband and ally George Butler, photographed during his tenure as Headmaster of Liverpool College. (Northumberland Archives)

Josephine poses in her prime to publicize the Ladies' National Association. (The Women's Library collection, LSE Library)

It appears from the Handbills issued by MR. CHILDERS
this morning, that

HE IS AFRAID TO MEET US,

And answer our questions on the Contagious Diseases Acts.

THEREFORE

M^{RS.} BUTLER

REQUESTS THE

WOMEN OF PONTEFRACT

TO MEET HER AT THE

LARGE ROOM, IN SOUTHGATE,

(USED BY MR. JOHNSON AS A SPINNING ROOM),

THIS EVENING AT SEVEN O'CLOCK.

MRS. BUTLER will shew that the Bill of which MR. CHILDERS
says he is now a supporter, while pretending to Repeal the "Contagious
Diseases Acts" is an extension of their principle to the whole country.
MRS. BUTLER will shew that MR. CHILDERS belongs to a
Government which has extended these Acts not only to this Country
but to the Colonies and Dependencies of the British Empire.
JOSEPHINE E. BUTLER, Hon. Sec. of the Ladies' National Association.

Ephemera from the Pontefract election campaign in 1872. Radically, Josephine is appealing for women to influence the vote. (The Women's Library collection, LSE Library)

Josephine at work in her parlour during the 1890s. (The Women's Library collection, LSE Library)

My dearest little Josephine

Aunt ❦ny is here. She brought with her a sweet little 🐱 in a 🧺 and Granny gives it 🥛 in a 🍽 and it sleeps in granny's 🛏 at night. Twice we lost it, but soon 🔔la found it again, sound asleep on a soft 🪑. There are some very pretty large 🌳 now in the gardens near which have pink flowers on them.

Old 🐕 curls dog went out with 🔔la, & ran into a pond and he went under the

Letters like this endeared 'Grannie' to the youngest members of her family. (John and David Thompson, courtesy of Helen Mathers)

The Butler family in 1897, including (back row, l-r) son Stanley, his wife Rhoda, Josephine, son Georgie (standing) and his wife Mia (holding the baby), son Charlie's wife Margaret and Charlie himself. (Northumberland Archives)

Artist Helen Whittaker has created a moving tribute to Josephine at the entrance of St Gregory the Great's church, Kirknewton. (© www.barryhale .co.uk, courtesy of Helen Whittaker)

she made should be based on solid evidence. And it was: so strong was her case against them, substantiated by Dyer, that both the Chief and his deputy were dismissed.

This did not mean that the trafficking ceased, however. As long as the supply chain remained open, girls would disappear from the homes and streets of Britain. It was an inconceivably shocking thought that boys were disappearing too, for the same purpose: Josephine was one of the few public figures brave enough to admit that this was so.

The same political dillydallying that delayed the Contagious Diseases Repeal Act also stymied legislation to raise the age of consent (material in combatting the slave trade). Dyer and Josephine were desperate for action. Josephine spoke and wrote about the subject, just as she had about the CDAs, while Dyer arranged an exposé of the procuress Mary Jeffries, an enterprising Londoner who ran brothels in such fashionable neighbourhoods as Chelsea, Kensington and Bloomsbury. Jeffries catered to clients with eclectic tastes in sadomasochism and paedophilia, outsourcing girls to the gentlemen's clubs of Mayfair and St James. According to Dyer, she counted among her clients four Lords, a Sir, an Honourable, a Consul, the King of the Belgians and the Prince of Wales.

When she was brought to trial in 1885, Jeffries pleaded guilty to the mildest possible charge of keeping a disorderly house (to avoid embarrassing disclosure of evidence) and was fined a paltry £200. Was the judiciary corrupt? Josephine felt impotent. 'I can forgive people longing for pistols who have not experienced the superior power of moral weapons,' she wrote. 'Indeed, at some moments I do also.'[2]

*

At times, Josephine Butler's life story seems a little too unlikely to be true. How on earth did this nice lady, born during the reign of George IV and brought up to live a sheltered life, end up a cutting-edge, uncompromising feminist for our times? What happened to her in 1885 looks more like a golden age silent movie than reality. Imagine a sad, doe-eyed heroine wringing her hands. 'My sisters are in mortal danger!' reads a decorated flashcard. A wholesome, Quakerish fellow tries to comfort her – that's Dyer – but the background music, increasingly turbulent, suggests he is not getting results. Then into the room sweeps a caped crusader, one fist in the air. As he leans against the closed door, another flashcard pops up (and the pianist changes key from minor to major). 'I shall tell the world and save you all!' Now the lady's hands are clasped to her breast as she gazes at the newcomer. 'My hero!'

In fact, William Stead was not Josephine's hero. She knew of him as a campaigning journalist, a supporter of the repealers, but for her taste, he indulged in too much 'holy gush'[3] and was over-keen on 'social purity' (or heavy-handed moral vigilance). In the campaign against trafficking, however, he was a powerful ally. As editor of the popular *Pall Mall Gazette*, his plan was to shock the public and Parliament into immediate legislation by producing a 'Special Report'. Josephine agreed to work with him.

On 4 July 1875, an editorial appeared in the *Pall Mall Gazette*, suggesting that 'all those who are prudish and all those who prefer to live in a fools' paradise of imagined innocence and purity . . . will do well not to read the *Pall Mall Gazette* of Monday and the following days.' So naturally, everyone did read it, though W. H. Smith refused to sell it on the grounds of obscenity. Stead's 'Special Report' ran for five days, entitled *The Maiden Tribute of Modern Babylon*, and told hair-raising stories of the underworld. There, virgins, or 'fresh girls', were bought from rapacious (or desperate) parents and then sold on 'guaranteed pure' by pimps; doctors and midwives were employed to examine such fresh girls to certify them intact; specialist brothels kept dozens of children under ten years old; Madams fitted out padded cells to stifle the screams of novice prostitutes; hardened women acted as decoys to lure the innocents into vice, and certain neighbourhoods were known for farming prostitutes for the open market.

At the heart of Stead's revelations was an elaborate sting involving Eliza Armstrong, a 13-year-old girl from Marylebone, London. For the purposes of this investigation, Stead arranged to purchase Eliza, paying her apparently compliant mother £1 – roughly £70 today – and a procuress who acted as broker another £4; then he had her virginity medically certified and spirited her off to France. It was terrifyingly easy.

This was sickening, sensational stuff. Hundreds of readers cancelled their subscriptions, though hundreds more joined demonstrations and signed petitions for action to outlaw such horrors. Both Stead and Josephine threatened to expose the names of prominent connoisseurs of young virgins in the British Establishment, which must surely have sped the passing of the Criminal Law Amendment Act a month later, on 10 August 1885. Among other clauses, the age of consent was raised to 16, and it was made a criminal act to abduct a girl under 18.

On 2 September, Stead was prosecuted – ironically, under the terms of the new Act – for abducting Eliza Armstrong. Josephine was implicated in the crime: she had provided Stead with a 'rescued' procuress, Rebecca Jarrett, who had used her old contacts to lead him to Eliza. Josephine had also involved her Salvation Army friends Florence and Bramwell Booth, who helped harbour both Eliza and Rebecca. Mr Booth and Jarrett were arraigned alongside Stead and two other accomplices; Jarrett was sentenced to six months' imprisonment, Stead to three, and Booth was acquitted. Josephine, somehow, escaped prosecution.

In 1882, George had retired from Liverpool College at 62, seeing no hope of promotion either in education or the church. Luckily, William Gladstone was an admirer of this unassuming man and recommended him for the Canonry of Winchester Cathedral. It upset Josephine to have to close her House of Rest in Liverpool, but she continued her practical work as best she could in Winchester, opening another refuge and hospital not far from the Cathedral Close as soon as possible.

The sporadic ill health she had suffered from for most of her life now became a chronic (though still unspecific) condition, chiefly affecting her heart and lungs. Other ailments came and went with increasing frequency. She began to dread the thought of public speaking and overexertion. She joined the National Vigilance Association for the Repression of Criminal Vice and Immorality (NVA) – successor to the LNA – but distrusted members' tendency, like Stead's, to be overjudgemental and to equate people's worth to their apparent purity. After a few years, she resigned. She also resigned her membership of the Women's Liberal Federation in 1891 because of their repeated failure to pressurize the government into giving women a vote.

At a time, in her mid-sixties, when most people would be thinking of making life a little easier, Josephine launched new campaigns in place of old ones. The garrison towns of British India were still subject to their own CDAs until public protest, orchestrated partly by Josephine, forced the passing of the Cantonment Act of 1895, making the registration and examination of prostitutes illegal. Josephine had helped to arrange a dangerous fact-finding trip to India by two American women, Dr Kate Bushnell and Mrs Elizabeth Andrews. According to Josephine, 'no inquiry ever in the history of the world was more admirably conducted to a successful issue than theirs.'[4]

After 1890, Josephine made few public appearances, preferring to 'help with my pen'[5] instead. She continued to write books and pamphlets on subjects ranging from the Boer War to St Catharine of Siena, but inevitably moved out of the spotlight and in time, off the stage altogether. She never lost her acute political awareness, however, nor the urge to do what she could to change things for the better, whatever the scale of the problem. Everyone who knows her name is aware of the campaigns against the CDAs and human trafficking. They were heroic. What emphasizes her humanity, however, is the knowledge that she used to donate whatever 'trifle' she could to a local dogs' home; that her children used to festoon her beloved horse with daisy chains before she rode him; that she wrote cheerfully to the homosexual Oscar Wilde (again, convicted under the terms of the 1885 Criminal Law Amendment Act) to comfort him in prison because she imagined how much he loved company and thought he must be lonely. She was kind on so many levels.

*

Josephine was almost as good at correspondence as she was at public speaking, and she never shied away from addressing anyone – from queens to whores, prime ministers to poor working men. Members of her family received literally thousands of letters, often cherished like this one, written around 1899 not to a VIP, but to her 11-year-old grandson Andrew (known as Bob), about to receive his school report and rather worried about it.

> I shall look forward to seeing your report at Christmas. But if any little accident should prevent it being as good as you wish, you will not be discouraged; and neither will I, because I know you have done your best.[6]

At this stage in her life, her family occupied her more than it had ever done: something she regretted, not because she begrudged the time now, but because she wished she had spent more before. For George, it was too late. He collapsed while travelling with Josephine in France in 1890, having suffered from jaundice, pericarditis and pleurisy, and died the day after arriving home in England. Josephine wrote a loving biography of him, as she had of her father, perhaps expressing on the page what she failed to do enough in person. That is certainly what their son Georgie thought: he reproached Josephine for stealing his father's livelihood, his life force, for her own ends. One gets the impression he did not consider his mother malicious, just blindly single-minded.

Stanley married in 1885 and moved to St Andrews in Scotland as professor of natural philosophy at the university there. He and Rhoda presented Josephine and George with their first two grandchildren: another Josephine, and Bob. Georgie married his cousin Mia in 1893 – they had two daughters and a son – and Eva's closest sibling Charlie wed Margaret Talbot four years later. Josephine declared herself ready to help and support her children and their growing families whenever she was needed. Bob remembered her as a delightful 'Grannie', smiling and endlessly generous. She was never pious or tiresomely holy; always elegant (she had a favourite grey silk cloak trimmed with black lace, and she loved furs). She still played the piano beautifully, drew and enjoyed charades. She was prone to bright little bursts of extravagance. That silk cloak was expensive. She once dropped half a sovereign in a Salvation Army penny-collecting tin (for old time's sake?) and when Andrew mentioned wanting a chisel, she bought him an entire toolbox. He loved her dearly.

So did her sons and daughters-in-law, but she frustrated them. Why did she choose, after George's death, to live virtually out of a suitcase, shifting through a succession of lodgings around London and Cheltenham, alone but for her maid and a dog? There is no doubt Josephine could be obstinate, even perverse, but she was also afraid of being a burden and losing control. Solitude was hard work, but she was used to that – and 'God is good.'[7]

In 1903, Josephine poetically completed the circle of life by settling close to Ewart Park where Georgie and his children lived, only a mile or two from Milfield, where she was born. Georgie's wife Mia had now died; Josephine's apparent reluctance to nurse her daughter-in-law/niece through her final illness alienated her still further from her eldest son. She tried to explain to him that she was herself desperately ill at the time, but he could not accept what he saw as further proof of her self-obsession.

Josephine remained efficient and independent until the day she died. She wrote lists of her possessions, explaining how they should be disposed. She left instructions about her funeral (it was to be simple and humble) and her preferred burial place (by George's side in Winchester). She also sent messages to surviving friends and former colleagues asking them to destroy any personal letters of hers in their possession. In November 1903, 'A Final Word' was published in *The Shield*, organ of the LNA and now the NVA, with which she had been associated for more than 30 years. It was an envoi to her comrades, 'in case I may not be permitted to remain long among you,' urging them to hope, with her, for a better life in this world and the next.

With that, she laid down her pen. She continued to write to her family when she could, but her public life was over. Josephine died in her little house in snowy Wooler on Sunday 30 December 1906, aged 78. She was buried not with her husband in Winchester but in nearby Kirknewton churchyard, where her paternal grandparents lay. Only ten people were at the funeral on 3 January 1907: her beloved maid, her grandson Bob, George, the vicar and his daughters, and one or two employees from Ewart Park. Charlie was far away, having emigrated to Canada.

Historians have claimed that Georgie kept the ceremony secret and ignored Josephine's wishes to spite her. But family correspondence suggests that there was little alternative, given the appalling weather at the time and an outbreak of influenza (which prevented both Stanley and Josephine's old ally James Stuart from travelling). Georgie explained to his brother that she had recently changed her mind about interment at Winchester, given the trouble and expense involved, and was content to rest at Kirknewton. Did he have Stanley's blessing to go ahead and arrange a local funeral as soon as possible? Stanley replied by telegram, concurring. This was a joint decision. Some of Josephine's closest friends were hurt that they had no chance to pay their last respects, but she did insist that the less fuss there was when she died, the better. Georgie did what he could to honour her wishes.

There was a distressing change in Josephine's personality towards the end. The day before she died, Stanley's son Bob wrote to Georgie to tell him about two letters he had just received from Grannie.

> They are so full of hatred and accusation of mother [Josephine's daughter-in-law Rhoda] that I sent back a reply . . . which Josephine calls a 'stunner.' I told J.E.B. her letters were <u>brutal</u>. She must either be quite mad: or filled with a sudden fit of devouring <u>hate</u>!
>
> We expect an explosion; but I do not care. Mother hopes to have a talk with you soon. We have not shown the letters to Daddy, they might shake his brain.[8]

Stanley was more conciliatory when he wrote to Georgie the following day (presumably ignorant of Josephine's recent broadsides). 'Some of her later letters have been cruel and unjust in tone. But we must forget all that.' He said he was glad he never retaliated, though strongly tempted at times to do so. His wife Rhoda, however, could not forgive Josephine. Or not for a while. She admitted 'it will take time – so [I am] not going to Mass, as [you] can only do that if you forgive . . . and so Grannie haunts one after her death.'[9]

Meanwhile, as the new year dawned, eulogies began to blow in with the winter blizzards. No doubt the family was gracious, recognizing with growing conviction that Josephine, for all her human frailty, was – as James Stuart said – 'one of the great people of the world'. Her own epitaph is more telling: she described herself as a simple woman, invited by God to be 'the representative of the outcast'.[10] It was the greatest privilege of her life to accept.

Part 2

THE LEGACY

5

An almost ideal woman

When news of Josephine's death broke during the first week of 1907, there was disquiet over what some regarded as an undignified hustle to bury her. Once people read about her final illness in letters or newspaper columns, it was too late to attend the funeral or even to send a wreath. Her close friend Fanny Forsaith took this as a deliberate betrayal of a long-standing and loving relationship. 'The only excuse I can find for the sons is that they may be carrying out Mrs Butler's wishes . . . but it could never have been her wish that her dearest friends should be pained as so many will have been by these proceedings.'[1]

The family continued to insist to one another and everyone else that it *was* Josephine's wish; no apology was necessary. Why the brothers failed to send immediate telegrams to James Stuart, for example, or the Wilsons in Sheffield, is unclear. It is true that Stanley was ill and Georgie no doubt preoccupied, while Charlie was out of the picture, but their failure to contact Josephine's loved ones was easily construed as discourtesy at best and at worst, an insult to her memory. Perhaps they were still smarting over that 'sudden fit of devouring hate'.

Josephine was characteristically forthright about the disposition of her effects. She willed her estate of £394 3s 5d – around £30,000 today – to her three sons. Given her habit of spending money on her various missions, charities and grandchildren without thought for the future, it is slightly surprising that she left so much. Georgie, Stanley, Charlie and their families also inherited the reams of letters written to them by Josephine over the years, most of which do not survive, though some have found their way into public collections. A number of 'spiritual notebooks' and personal papers was retrieved from her rooms in Wooler, obviously written for family members, with quavery inscriptions like 'for George Grey Butler [Georgie] to keep and to read whenever he pleases' or 'a record of some family events and of God's goodness to me'.[2] It is a sign of her obsession with privacy that when she no longer felt able to write in longhand and was forced to employ a 'confidential lady typist' from an agency, she insisted that the woman should not know who had commissioned her. Nor did Josephine want to know her name.

Towards the end of her life, Josephine listed her most precious possessions.[3] It is touching to read what she chose to keep when embarking on her itinerant life after George's death: an 'old-fashioned but rather valuable' inlaid table of her mother's (to remain at Ewart Park after her death); an easel and paintbox given to her by George (for her grandson Bob); her beloved grand piano (left to granddaughter Hetha); a cherished lock of Eva's hair, together with the child's thimble and needle case (for Charlie).

To her friends, she left a strict injunction. No personal memoir should *ever* be written of her, no private correspondence made public and no ink wasted on high-flown eulogies.

I have long disliked and deprecated the prevailing and somewhat morbid habit – borrowed largely from America – of laying open to the public every detail of the inner life of men and women whose names have been at all known, and an analysis of the character of the person dealt with which [is] far from true . . . I cannot help feeling that it is above all unseemly to endeavour to probe and to expose to the public the spiritual life and experience of those who are gone.[4]

She realized that a certain amount of fuss would be inevitable when she died, given her former celebrity; she did not relish the idea, but there it was. On no account, however, should anyone be allowed to discuss her personality or presume to understand her relationship with God, whether they knew her in life or not. (*Mea culpa*, Josephine.) Other than turn in her grave, there was nothing she could do to enforce the embargo. Her legacy was too valuable to dissipate in obscurity.

Obituaries came thick and fast. Letters of condolence written to the family spoke of Josephine as someone who moulded history, heroic, a social reformer of towering influence and a human being of rare humility. She was 'the greatest woman of our time, if greatness be measured by nobility of spirit',[5] whose loss was more than a personal blow; it diminished the nation.

Journalists – on the whole - were inclined to agree.

Mrs Butler is described by one of her fellow-workers as 'an almost ideal woman; devoted wife, exquisitely human and feminine, with no touch in her of the 'woman of the platform,' though with a great gift of pleading speech, with a powerful mind, and a soul purged through fire.[6]

That is from *The Times*. *The London Daily News* recalled her work in Liverpool, marked by numerous discreet acts of kindness. She once arranged and paid for a dying prostitute to travel home to Staffordshire, for instance, to make peace with her father before she died. An admirer from East Sussex wrote to his local paper about meeting Josephine in Switzerland back in the 1870s. She had a nervous twitch in her fingers 'which never ceased for a moment',[7] he remembered. This was not a sign of weakness, but sheer intensity.

The Inverness Courier thought it disgraceful that she was tucked away in a remote country churchyard: she should have been given a resting place in Westminster Abbey. *The Newcastle Daily Chronicle* cited her as a perfect example of the power of popular democracy, 'displaying great ability, unflinching courage, and the persistency of conviction which is unmoved by misrepresentation . . . The Mary Wollstonecraft of the Victorian Era'.[8]

Misrepresentation was something Josephine had faced for much of her life; it followed her in death. A few newspapers recorded the demise of 'the widow of the late Canon Butler', coyly noting that she had 'interested herself in certain social questions' and hardly crediting her as an individual at all. She was witheringly described elsewhere as a 'well-known lady publicist' with no self-respect; a 'mistaken' eccentric who had had her day, 'little known to the present generation' and 'almost forgotten'. However, the majority celebrated Josephine as someone who changed lives for the better; someone beautiful who fought ugliness; someone frail whose strength was irresistible; a rebel born and bred.

*

In April 1907, a crowded meeting was held at Caxton Hall in Westminster to commemorate the life and work of Josephine Butler. It was a chance for those who had missed her funeral three months earlier to pay their respects. James Stuart presided; Catherine Bramwell Booth, daughter of the Salvation

Army's founders, was also there, with suffragist leader Millicent Fawcett. On the stage was a mournful portrait of Josephine surrounded by palm leaves. That same year, her name was added to a memorial in the Dissenters' section of Kensal Green cemetery for those who 'defied custom and interest for the sake of conscience and the public good'. The following summer, members of the National Union of Women's Suffrage Societies carried aloft a huge blue-and-gold banner emblazoned with her name in a procession through London. When the fight for the vote was won (partially) in 1918, she was honoured at the celebrations as one of the campaign's pioneers.

Meanwhile, agencies in Liverpool were busy gathering support for a training school to be set up in her name. Josephine Butler Memorial House was opened in 1920, just a mile or so away from the Brownlow Hill workhouse. Four years later, it moved to larger premises in Abercrombie Square, at the heart of the University of Liverpool, with which it was linked. It prepared women for a career in welfare work, which would surely have made Josephine proud, though the Bishop of Liverpool's stipulation that at least two thirds of its students must be Anglicans might not have pleased her quite so much. She always hated the divisiveness of labels.

The year 1928 was a landmark year for feminists. Ten weary years after the Representation of the People Act gave the vote to women over 30, the so-called Equal Franchise Act was passed. At last – more than half a century after Josephine had signed John Stuart Mill's petition in 1866 – women were allowed to vote on the same terms as men. Sadly, stalwart suffragette Emmeline Pankhurst died a month too soon to witness the end of the struggle.

The year 1928 also marked the centenary of Josephine's birth. The vaguely sinister-sounding Association of Moral and Social Hygiene put itself in charge of the celebrations. (It had been formed in 1915 as an amalgamation of the LNA and the International Abolitionist Federation. Less repressive than the National Vigilance Association, it campaigned for gender equality in matters of sexual morality and legislation.) A centenary committee was formed to organize suitable events across the country, supported by a raft of VIPs. Eighty-year-old Millicent Fawcett was Honorary Secretary; others involved included Liverpudlian Eleanor Rathbone MP, writer John Galsworthy, prominent Oxford academics Michael Sadler and Margery Fry, the Archbishop of York, and the first Labour Prime Minister, Ramsay MacDonald.

Meetings honouring Josephine's life and work were held in Westminster Abbey, Manchester Central Hall, Newcastle, Sheffield and elsewhere, with banners, hymns and speeches. Special pamphlets were published about 'the most heroic and sympathetic figure of the nineteenth century'. In one of them, Fawcett listed the ongoing fruits of Josephine's labours. A Royal Commission on VD (1913–1916) had denounced the regulation of prostitution. In 1925, a Colonial Office Advisory Committee 'utterly condemned as medically useless' periodic examination of prostitutes. A League of Nations Report published its findings on the sex trafficking of women and children in 1927, and that same year, a government committee was appointed to enquire into the operation of the Solicitation Laws. 'She has changed the outlook of the whole Western World in regard to standards of sex-morality,' concluded Fawcett.[9]

Back in the 1870s, the famous French author Victor Hugo sent a fist-pumping message to Josephine to sustain her in the fight against the CDAs. 'I am with you, Madame and ladies. I am with you to the fullest extent of my power . . . Protest!

Resist!' The message was revived by the Association of Moral and Social Hygiene in 1928, partly in recognition of Josephine, but also to try to rally a new generation of activists to the Cause. There was still work to be done. State-regulated prostitution persisted in pockets of British territories abroad; there remained a moral double standard of expectation and culpability in sexual matters, and the trafficking of women and children continued, to everyone's shame. Campaigners hoped that the centenary would not only honour an old crusader, but invigorate an army of younger ones to cleanse the world of vice, once and for all.

But was that the chief concern of Josephine's campaign? Or was it more about compassion, justice, treating one's neighbour as oneself? To the Butlers – especially as time healed – she was simply a loving, holy, tireless and infinitely inspiring member of the family; the ultimate role-model. When the centenary committee wrote to Bob to ask for help with a speech for the Westminster Abbey event, he replied (marking his letter 'very private' – old habits die hard) with a heartfelt personal tribute. His grandmother's greatest assets, he reckoned, were her natural generosity; her sense of humour and delight in the ridiculous; her clear, strong faith ('not the least churchy'); her assumption of goodness in everybody, which she usually found; and above all, her humility.[10]

These qualities were more lustrous than any legacy of gold or jewels, books or letters, deeds or words. They summed up who Josephine was and informed everything she achieved in a life remarkable by any standard.

6

Portraits in words and pictures

For someone who claimed that words heard on the platform were far more powerful than those read on the page, Josephine was an extraordinarily prolific author. It is difficult to count accurately, when shoals of minor publications are apt to slip through the net like minnows attendant on bigger fish, but a reasonable tally appears to be about 46 major printed works.[1] Their subjects are broadly categorized as social welfare, feminism, biography and memoir, and religion, but the boundaries between them can be fluid. They are largely well written: controlled, but with an obvious flair for the dramatic.

Though sentimental at times, her work very rarely tends towards sanctimony or (as her grandson was proud to note) towards preachiness. Sentimentality was the spirit of the age, after all; Josephine was quite capable of capturing tender hearts for the benefit of her crusade. Incisive publications like *The Education and Employment of Women* and *Woman's Work and Woman's Culture* were groundbreaking, not saccharine at all. We must conclude that Josephine was a skilled communicator of the written as well as what she called the 'living' word: aware of her target audience (sympathetic men and hesitant women – or vice versa) and slickly persuasive.

Her choice of biographical subjects is interesting. She published lives of family heroes: her father, sister Hatty and husband George, to honour them and – in the latter case, one suspects – to expiate for any real or perceived shortcomings on her part. She also wrote about the French social alchemist Johann Oberlin (1740–1846), who created vibrant, prosperous communities from some of most deprived villages in the Vosges. Her *tour de force* in this field, however, is a biography of Catherine of Siena (1878): surely her favourite saint, who rose elegantly from uneducated obscurity in the fourteenth century to counsel princes and popes.

Inevitably, the book you are reading now is not the first to have ignored Josephine's explicit wishes about the publication of her own life story by anyone other than herself. She tried to satisfy the appetite for such a publication by producing *Personal Reminiscences of a Great Crusade* (1896), which – though ostensibly about the campaign against the CDAs – did offer carefully engineered glimpses of herself and other members of the Grey and Butler clans. But it was too little, too late.

Ever the canny journalist, William Stead published a 'Life Sketch' in 1888, riding on the back of the publicity caused by *The Maiden Tribute of Modern Babylon* and the repeal of the CDAs. Josephine was not amused, being a firm opponent of Stead's peculiar brand of self-righteous sensationalism. An 'Autobiographical Memoir' – a collection of Josephine's own writings edited by fellow abolitionists George and Lucy Johnson – came out in 1909, and a 'Cameo Life Sketch', published by the Women's Freedom League as propaganda for the suffrage campaign, in 1913. Very deliberately, no one had yet used the 'b' word.

Millicent Fawcett's book on Josephine appeared in time for the centenary. Written in collaboration with Miss E. M. Turner of the Association for Moral and Social Hygiene, *Josephine Butler: Her Work and Principles* (1927) is not strictly a biography at all. In fact, it was not until 1954 that the first authorized life appeared, written by Josephine's grandson Bob (architect A. S. G. Butler). *Portrait of Josephine Butler* is a delightful book – though not always factually accurate – bringing to life everyone's idea of a favourite grandparent. She steps lightly through the pages, stylish, fragrant, twinkly and fun, dispensing ridiculously indulgent alms to passing beggars and quirky gifts to young relatives. She is wise, impassioned and obviously enjoys a direct line to God.

By this time, Octavia Hill's biographer Enid Moberly Bell had been petitioning the Butlers for years for permission to write the first full-length, independent life of Josephine. They refused; eventually, Moberly Bell went ahead anyway with *Josephine Butler: Flame of Fire* in 1962, which remained the definitive biography until Jane Jordan's was published in 2001.

One wonders what Josephine was afraid of. She courted useful publicity and, as far as we know, had very little to hide during her active years. Yet her abhorrence of intrusion into her personal and spiritual life bordered on the obsessive. It could be that her own explanation was the true one: that she did not feel important enough to warrant the interest, and that a misdirection of attention on Josephine Butler the celebrity compromised the effectiveness of Josephine Butler the campaigner.

Somehow that does not ring quite true. Were they not the same thing? Besides, she was highly self-aware in terms of appearance and dress, as anxious to please as is anyone who looks for the best in others. It smacks of a certain brand of pride to demand exclusive privacy, yet Josephine was truly humble. Perhaps this was more about God and her family than about her. '[T]he present is such a <u>shouting</u> age, such a self-advertising age,' she wrote to a friend in 1903, 'which to me seems removed from the spirit of Christ.'[2] She would have hated Christ to think her arrogant and hated her family now or in the future to think her exploitative in any way. She considered it her duty to be discreet, even after death.

*

Josephine once claimed to despise photographs almost as much as she despised the wrong sort of publicity. They made her look so miserable, she said. '[E]very attempt has stamped upon the face such an expression of profound melancholy . . . as wholly belies my character.'[3] She curated photographic portraits carefully, choosing affirmative images to mark the different stages of her working life. None of them lacks a certain glamour. In youth and middle age, she tends to be seated with the left side of her face towards the camera, her right hand held to her chin, looking down at a book or serenely ahead. These are thoughtful, sympathetic poses, emphasizing her aristocratic profile (rather like Virginia Woolf's) and dignified femininity. She appears to be listening, strong but unthreatening.

There are exceptions to this scenario. A joint portrait taken with husband George soon after he had been ordained has Josephine standing rigid behind his chair in a pale, printed dress, leaning in towards him and looking startled. Another image was taken by fashionable photographers Elliott and Fry in 1886, when the CDAs were repealed. There, she stands as if just about to stride forward and attend briskly to the next item of business.

Her hair is always loosely coiffed, sometimes (in her younger days) with a ringlet or two resting on her shoulder. As she ages, her headdresses grow more elaborate: a strange, feathery turban; a cross between a nun's wayward wimple and a sheikh's gutra;

a flowing lace veil. She is usually wearing a heavy necklace or two and long earrings and is dressed in thick, dark clothes with self-coloured satin bows or frogging. The archives at Liverpool University possess some of her jewellery, glossy black pieces of Whitby jet (traditionally signifying mourning), together with some hat pins, ivory glove-stretchers, and a pair of spectacles – which do not appear in any photographs I have seen. Spectacles send the wrong message.

Images taken in her later years reveal someone who looks as though she is constantly shivering – wrapped up against the cold, serious and somewhat stiff – except for one in the collections of the Women's Library in London with the handwritten caption 'Grannie thinking what she is going to write in her book'. She sits at a book-strewn table covered in a comfortably cluttered parlour, holding a pen, gazing towards the window and *almost* smiling.

Paintings can often be more eloquent than photographs. Early depictions of Josephine look fairly generic: a conventionally attractive young woman in watercolours or oils with smooth hair parted in the middle and liquid eyes. Society artist George Richmond made a chalk drawing of her in 1851, probably to mark her engagement. It was exciting sitting for him, according to Josephine: 'he is a capital talker, & very witty & amusing, & knows all the great nobs, having taken their likenesses.'[4] Though he famously and successfully drew novelists Charlotte Brontë and Elizabeth Gaskell, his sketch of Josephine looks slightly insipid.

The LNA used to sell plaster copies and postcard reproductions of a bust of Josephine to raise funds. The original was sculpted by Alexander Munro in 1855-1856, one of a pair. The other, in marble, is at Girton College, Cambridge. Newnham College might have been a more appropriate home, given that Josephine was one of its founders in the days when she was associated with the North of England Council for Promoting the Higher Education of Women. But George Butler's sister-in-law Agnata Butler chose to leave it to her own *alma mater*. She offered it to the National Portrait Gallery first; presumably, they turned it down. It is almost life-sized, and though its subject is immediately recognizable (that nose, and the pre-Raphaelite hair), she does look incongruously coquettish. Her thin chiton, or Greek tunic, has slipped from a shoulder, leaving it provocatively bare, and there is an alluring challenge in her tilted chin and level, blank-eyed stare. Josephine was delighted with Munro's work, however, commissioning him to sculpt a marble and serpentine plaque of Eva cradling a dove soon after the child's death.

The next – and last – formal likeness of Josephine was an oil painting produced by George Watts as part of his suite of eminent Victorians, a kind of Hall of Fame, in 1895. She was the only woman included in this parade of reformers; Florence Nightingale was supposed to be joining Josephine but Watts never got around to finishing her. The artist was 78 when Josephine sat for him; she was 67. It is a very dark painting. Josephine's face peers from a background of deep browns and black, her expression hovering between gloom and despair.[5] It was not thought to be a great success by the gallery-going public, but for Josephine herself, it held a strange fascination, despite what she had formerly said about cheerless photographs.

She wrote to the artist to explain how she felt when she saw the finished work.

My dear Mr Watts,

I want to tell you in writing what it is difficult to say in words. When I looked at that portrait which you have just done, I felt inclined to burst into tears. I will tell you why. I felt sorry for her. Your power has brought up, out of the depths of the past, the record of a conflict which no one but God knows of. It is written in the eyes and in the whole face. There were years in which my revolt was, not against man, but against God; my soul went down to hell, and dwelt there. It was a woe which has left its marks, long after peace had been restored, just as an old tree bears the marks of a storm by which it was blasted long ago altho' the weather is so calm now that not a leaf stirs.

Your picture has brought back to me all that I suffered and all the sorrow through which the Angel of God's presence brought me out alive. I thank you that you have not made that poor woman look severe or bitter, but only sad, and yet purposeful. For with full purpose of heart she has borne and laboured, and she is ready to go down into Hades again, if it were necessary for the deliverance of her fellow-creatures. But God does not require that descent more than once. I could not say all this aloud. But if the portraiture speaks with such truth and power to me, I think it will in some way speak to others also.

Yours gratefully,
Josephine E. Butler.[6]

It *did* speak to others, but more of sadness than anything else. Much more uplifting are two posthumous images of Josephine in stained-glass windows. The first is in Liverpool's Anglican Cathedral, one of a series of 'noble women' in the Lady Chapel; the other is at St Olave's Church in Hart Street, London, where she shines gently in the company of Florence Nightingale, Elizabeth Fry and Edith Cavell, bathed – at last – in light and colour.

7

Ignorance is not bliss

Josephine Butler's influence on her world was far-reaching. As one of the most famous women of her age, and a pioneer in multiple fields – spiritual, social, educational and political – it would not be an exaggeration to say she made an impact on the lives of hundreds of thousands of people. It is difficult to think of any woman before her with such authority.

Take spirituality first. Most middle-class parlours in the second half of the nineteenth century were adorned with elaborately decorated mottoes like 'Prepare to Meet Thy God', 'The Meek Shall Inherit the Earth', 'Watch and Pray'. While Josephine spent her whole life preparing to meet her God, she was not particularly interested in inheriting the earth or in watching and praying without doing. Nor did she subscribe to the idiom of a spiritual hierarchy that imagined women demurely hesitant on the lower rungs of a ladder to heaven, while men, by divine right, shinned ahead. 'The Church has always allowed herself to be bound, held back, dragged down, more or less, by the overpowering weight of unregenerate male feeling.'[1] This was a dangerously provocative thing to say. That is why she said it. After all, the best way to change public opinion is to challenge it.

Josephine refused to be labelled an Anglican, or anything else. Her idiosyncratic brand of Christianity was inclusive, socialist in its egalitarianism and forbearance (though she appeared far more ready to excuse wayward women than misguided men). We are humans first, she said, men and women next, and our souls have identical value in the sight of the Lord, whether or not we are outwardly virtuous. There is no place for a pecking order in a modern, enlightened religion. Pre-empting Mary Baker Eddy, who popularized the concept in Christian Science, Josephine even went so far as to speak of 'the Great Father-Mother God,'[2] implying that there was no place for gender discrimination, either.

One of Josephine's greatest assets was her ability to discuss shocking subjects in a calm, persuasive way. That is how she was able to sustain such progressive arguments about personal morality without being dismissed (entirely) as subversive, a madwoman or some kind of witch. She had her enemies, as we have seen, who considered her blasphemous and possibly dangerous too, and who subscribed to the traditional adage that for *nice* ladies, ignorance was bliss. But the majority of her readers and listeners credited her at the very least with sincerity. She was so patently well-meaning. To a great extent, that overrode her unorthodoxy and perhaps eased the way for other nonconformists (in a general rather than a sectarian sense) to be given a fair hearing. She was tolerant, so evinced tolerance in others.

Her nephew Charles Grey was certain that had Josephine chosen to convert to Roman Catholicism, 'she would probably have been canonized, or sanctified or whatever they call it . . . as St Josephine of Milfield.'[3] It was enough for her to claim Christ as a close and long-suffering friend who would welcome her into the Kingdom with a smile and quiet congratulations for having done her very best. She once said that the main object of her life had been to fight against injustice – job done.

Turning to social matters: that fight yielded practical as well as ideological results. Figures released shortly before the Second World War revealed that the incidence of VD in the British Army fell from 246 per 1000 during the operation of the CDAs to 9 per 1000 after their repeal.[4] Not only that; measures to mitigate 'vice' – inspired by the LNA's campaign – had resulted in better recreational, educational, economic and social conditions for everyone serving in His Majesty's Forces, at home and overseas. And the civil population benefited too. Ministry of Health statistics published in 1933 showed a 24 per cent reduction in VD cases overall and a 51 per cent drop in syphilis alone.[5] This was indirectly due to Josephine having the courage to articulate the problem in the first place (and so break the taboo), then campaigning for change and encouraging less judgmental, more humane clinical treatment for male 'consumers' as well as women 'providers.'

A raft of legislation developed in the wake of the LNA's crusades against the CDAs and sex trafficking. Certain achievements stand out: raising the age of consent for girls and boys to 16, setting the age for marriage at 16 from 12 for girls and 14 for boys (staggeringly, this did not happen until 1929), and changing the law on the definition and implications of illegitimacy, reducing the inevitable stigma and economic disadvantages involved. In 1933, Great Britain signed an international convention against sex trafficking, acting on a problem virtually hidden from public view before Josephine and William Stead placed it firmly in the limelight. Other legislation was put in place to tackle the social conditions forcing women onto the streets in the first place.

Josephine's legacy as an educationalist was to encourage intellectual curiosity in respectable adult women through her support of the University Extension scheme, to equip schoolgirls with a benchmark qualification for higher education by campaigning for nationwide examinations, and to help provide a safe space at Cambridge for female undergraduates to learn at the highest possible level. In so doing, she raised the expectations of teachers and students alike.

Finally, politics. She and her abolitionist colleagues were among the first in Europe to demonstrate that it was possible for women to organize themselves into an effective and well-administrated body. It was not customary before this for crowds of them to meet together with a common purpose in mind, to elect their own officers, write their own agendas and minute their own conclusions. This was democracy in the making. The LNA was arguably the first such body to effect political change, setting a crucial precedent for the success of the campaign for women's suffrage. At the heart of all of Josephine's activism was the necessity for women to find a voice and use it well. For voice, read vote.

It follows that she was the first female politician to take to a public platform as though it were her natural habitat, to perfect the art and science of public speaking and therefore to become a celebrity not because of who she was, but what she said. At her best, she was a consummate performer, whose audiences spanned class, generation, gender, political allegiance and religion.

*

Members of the LNA and subsequent women's associations would be the first to admit that, collectively, they could not have accomplished what they did without sympathetic male champions, just as individually, Josephine and other wives and mothers relied on the encouragement of their menfolk (thus turning upside down the trope of a wife sacrificing all for her husband). Josephine never forgot the blessing George gave her – 'Go! And the Lord be with you' – when she first confessed to him the distasteful nature of her vocation in 1870. The campaign against the CDAs united men and women both practically and philosophically. Josephine invited the co-operation of all comers. She was keen to make the point that like the fight for the vote, it was never about 'them' and 'us'. It was not a war between the sexes, but a joint campaign against a common enemy: the state regulation of vice.

This acknowledgement of male support did not prevent Josephine from pulling a few extremely hard-hitting feminist punches. She might not have been called a feminist then, of course; the term only came into common usage shortly before her death. But we can recognize the signs. Quoting the political scientist Alexis de Tocqueville, she wrote in 1874 that 'nothing is more customary in man than to recognize superior wisdom in the person of his oppressor.' In other words, it is often easier to act as though one deserves discrimination than to challenge it. De Tocqueville was talking about slaves, but Josephine made the point that he might just as well have been talking about women.[6] It was time to rise up against that oppressor (a patriarchal state) by shaming him into capitulation.

Even more outrageous was her indictment of imperialism: 'There is no creature in the world so ready as the Englishman to destroy, to enslave, to domineer, and to grow fat upon the destruction of the weaker human beings whom he has subjected to his bold and iron will.'[7] But it was no good bleating about it, advised Josephine; right-thinking women must somehow take charge of their own destiny. That right-thinking women *had* a destiny other than daughterhood followed by wifehood followed by motherhood followed by death was a revelation to many.

That was a stereotype she shattered herself, being both feminine and proactive; respectable and a rebel. She turned the domestic model inside out (literally), enjoying a higher public profile than her husband and relying on him being at home for her to function in the world. She used a political voice she was not supposed to have, to claim legal and human rights she was not supposed to recognize. She pioneered the concept of sisterly solidarity, of quiet deeds speaking louder than words, of changing the world one voice at a time. She opened the discussion on gender equality in the workplace, the church pew, the law court and the marriage bed. She claimed there was no morality without personal freedom and that morality itself should not be quantified as an economic but a spiritual imperative. In short, she challenged us to listen unhindered to our consciences and make the world a kinder, fairer place for everyone.

In 1962, a new pressure group was set up to continue some of the work and ideals of the LNA and its immediate successor, the Association for Moral and Social Hygiene. Josephine's campaigns against gender inequality and sexual exploitation remained live, changing focus as society evolved through war and peace. Then, as the age of freely available contraception and 'women's lib' approached, activists judged it more important to keep women safe in a sexualized society than to struggle for some sort of moral utopia. To put it another way: members of the LNA had hoped to elevate men's morality (which they considered flawed and easily corrupted by economic greed) to match women's (innately yearning for purity and fidelity). The new association was more pragmatic, promoting a single standard of sexual responsibility and supporting agencies to help those tempted into – or trying to escape from – prostitution.

What should they call it? It was intended to represent a breath of fresh air, addressing modern problems but in that old, pioneering spirit. One could have too much of acronyms, and references to 'moral hygiene' or 'purity' were off-putting. So they returned to basics. It was named the Josephine Butler Society, and it still exists.

Whether Josephine herself would have been satisfied with the remit of her namesake society is an interesting question. She had the highest moral standards personally, and though unusually forgiving, believed that with Christ's help, everyone – male or female – should strive to lead a morally unimpeachable life. When they achieved that, they would be free to create a joyful society governed by the laws of natural justice, where everyone was given the opportunity to flourish in mind and body.

By a morally unimpeachable life she meant a traditionally Christian one, which in her era required strict sexual continence. But she was a pragmatist, too. Who knows: had she been born a century later, she might well have campaigned for safety over celibacy, and free love over bounden duty (given that the two were not indivisible, which for Victorian Christians was debatable). What is important is that she created an open, airy climate for the critical examination of issues previously swathed in a chauvinistic smog of denial. Josephine threw open society's windows to let in the light.

8

Do not imagine you are powerless

The Cheviot Hills reach around the church of St Gregory the Great in Kirknewton as though holding it in a loose embrace. Josephine's grave is to the left of the porch, west of the squat bell tower. It is neat and unobtrusive. An area of gravel is enclosed by a low boundary. A horizontal cross lies in the centre, as long as Josephine was tall. The olive-green stone is mottled with grey and yellow lichen, so much so that the original memorial plate is almost illegible. A more recent one is easier to read: 'Josephine Butler, Social Reformer, 1828-1906. To the memory of Josephine Elizabeth Butler, Widow of George Butler, Canon of Winchester Cathedral, and Daughter of John Grey of Milfield.' So we know to whom she belonged, but not who she was. The only other information given is the exact date of her death and her age. It all seems a little stark.

Retrace your steps to the porch, and you will find a more fitting tribute. A sculpture by Helen Whittaker was installed there in 2006 to mark the centenary of Josephine's birth – and baptism at this same church – incorporating limpid, coloured glass; copper lilies and bindweed, and the words 'She loved, she prayed, she endured.' It is exquisite.

The Church of England celebrates what is called a 'lesser festival' on the anniversary of her baptism on 30 May. This means special prayers are told in her memory:

God of compassion and love, by whose grace your servant Josephine Butler followed in the way of your Son in caring for those in need: help us like her to work with strength for the restoration of all to the dignity and freedom of those created in your image . . .

God our redeemer, who inspired Josephine Butler to witness to your love and to work for the coming of your kingdom: may we, who in this sacrament share the bread of heaven, be fired by your Spirit to proclaim the gospel in our daily living and never to rest content until your kingdom come, on earth as it is in heaven; through Jesus Christ our Lord.

The ceremony is particularly dear to the Kirknewton congregation.

A few miles away at Wooler, the semi-detached house where Josephine died has a metal plaque on the wall, erected by the local Women's Institute. It honours an individual who, like the founders of the WI, realized the importance of equipping women in every walk of life with knowledge. Knowledge leads to understanding; understanding leads to responsibility; and responsibility, to reform. The farmhouse where Josephine was born, at the village of Milfield, was demolished in the 1960s, but Georgie and Mia's place, Ewart Park, still stands like a miniature stately home – though empty at the time of writing, and rather sad. There are English Heritage blue plaques marking Josephine's residence at Cheltenham and Wimbledon Common, and a local brown plaque at the site of her House of Rest in Liverpool, commemorating her as a moral crusader.[1]

Her name lives on elsewhere. The Josephine Butler Care Home for the elderly is a couple of miles away from the House of Rest. An annual Josephine Butler award is made by the Diocese of Liverpool to celebrate the achievements of community activists. There is a Josephine Butler primary school in Northumberland. There is even a beer named after her by a Liverpool brewery: 'initial citrus hops [are] followed by elderflower fruit and pale, biscuit malt with a refreshing sharp finish.' And in 2006, 'Josephine Butler College' opened at Durham University, where George Butler once taught and, possibly, where he met his wife for the first time. It is the university's youngest college and home to some 400 young men and women who probably take their right to higher education entirely for granted. The college is described on its website as 'free-spirited, flourishing and full of life.' That sounds about right. At the height of her powers, Josephine was all of those.

*

The first stop for any student of Josephine's life and work must be the archive of the Josephine Butler Society in London. It includes an exhaustive collection of printed material by and about her, as well as the Society's official papers. It was originally deposited in the Fawcett Society Library, founded by her friend Millicent Fawcett and dedicated (as it still is) to social justice for women. In 1998, the archive was transferred to the Women's Library at the LSE, and it is accessible – by prior arrangement – to all.

Fashions change in scholarship as often as they do on the High Street. Apart from the previously mentioned biographies by Bob Butler and Enid Moberly Bell, nothing much was written about Josephine *the person* between the 1930s and 1960s. This was nothing to do with lingering deference to her wish for privacy; Victorian personalities were simply out of vogue, especially if they were female. What mattered was not who people were, but what they represented. Josephine appeared as a cipher for the ladies' campaign against the CDAs, a cardboard cut-out popping up from the footnotes with an angry face and a pointy finger.

During the 1970s, when social history emerged as a valid academic discipline, the focus changed. Papers were published on the work of Josephine in her cultural context, on her activism in all its guises and on its effect on her own life and others'. Since then, she has been labelled variously as 1) a politician, one of the architects of women's suffrage; 2) a feminist, who first awoke women to the possibility of agency (the quote at the head of this chapter – 'do not imagine you are powerless' – is taken from her *Letter to the Mothers of England*, 1881); 3) an evangelist, who lived and breathed her faith every moment of every day; and 4) (it takes all sorts) a maverick whose precarious mental health and sublimated sexuality drove her to extremes. And plenty of other things, too. She has been cast as a woman of her time, a woman ahead of her time, a woman of today.

That last role is intriguing. We might think the #MeToo movement is something new; Josephine thought of it before us, demanding an end to sexual harassment and gender stereotyping. We might think intersectional feminism is new; again, Josephine was familiar with the theory, acknowledging the multiple disadvantages of various women she met in Brownlow Hill Bridewell, for example. The accepted wisdom at the time was that they were there because they were criminals, and society must therefore guard against them. Josephine maintained that the problem was more complex. What led up to their incarceration? Were they there because they were poor? Abused? Terrified of someone or hopelessly in love? Addicted to alcohol or opiates? Or just plain immoral? And *why* were they any of these things in this modern, enlightened world? Her implicit answer: because women did not have the political voice or the education to change things, and not enough people listened to Christ.

Josephine was a pioneering whistle-blower. In the 1980s, gynaecologist Professor Wendy Savage was dismissed from her post at the London Hospital Medical School on the grounds of incompetence. She believed in her patients' prerogative to choose where and how to give birth or whether to have an abortion. Because she was an outspoken, opinionated woman, standing up for what she believed to be her patients' human rights, she was easily characterized by a largely male establishment as a troublemaker. So was Josephine Butler. The two women may have had vastly different outlooks on sexual and religious morality, but both of them were passionate about empowering females to make decisions about their own bodies.

In 1997, Jayne Senior, a youth worker in Rotherham, South Yorkshire, set up a project for vulnerable young women between 11 and 25 called Risky Business. In the course of her work, she helped uncover horrific evidence of the systematic sexual exploitation of around 1,400 girls between 1997 and 2013. Local authorities had cause to suspect the abuse but failed to act, according to the official enquiry led by (female) Professor Alexis Jay. The abusers were eventually brought to justice with convictions for rape, conspiracy to rape, false imprisonment and conspiracy to procure prostitutes. Two of the accused were women. How Josephine would have wept for their victims – the very same victims she and William Stead struggled so hard to protect in 1886.

Josephine's written work is full of toothsome soundbites. She was an accomplished rhetorician and knew as well as any modern media savant how to lodge a message in someone's consciousness. The 'father-mother God' quote is one of the most memorable. Following the ordination in 2015 of the first female bishop in the Anglican Church, there was a call from progressive theologians to change the liturgy. Why should God be addressed exclusively as a male? It was alienating. Female pronouns were suggested, and are indeed in use in some congregations, but they have failed to catch on. Maybe

Josephine's startling suggestion of the 'father-mother' God is the way to go? Political correctness gone mad, or true inclusivity? You tell me. Josephine was nothing if not provocative.

She once suggested that there is no such thing as a necessary evil. That was a shocking thing to say to a Christian society brought up on biblical stories of Satan and hell. So was her stern assertion that Christian behaviour was not a matter of picking out the plums and leaving the rotten fruit to someone else. 'I am not here to represent virtuous women. I plead for the rights of the most virtuous and the most vicious equally.'[2]

In 1888, she wrote this: 'the women of the world are reaching out their hands to each other and banding themselves together.'[3] That is an expression of sisterhood that would be recognized by anyone at the Greenham Common Peace Camp in the 1980s and 1990s, or joining a Million Women March recently. Arguably, Josephine *invented* sisterhood, in the political sense. What a gift.

Reducing the work and life of an individual to a single concept is an invidious business, even for a biographer, but if there is one live lesson to be learned from Josephine Butler, it must surely be that mutual support lies at the heart of social change. With this in mind, here is a final image of the strength and compassion of a woman remarkable in so many ways, described in a letter written by her in 1888.[4] She is on the platform at a mass meeting. The audience is predominantly female, but there are men there as well. They listen spellbound to what she has to say about the brutal treatment inflicted on women by the operation of the CDAs – women she has met and can name. When she has finished her speech, all passion spent, there is silence.

Then, at first one by one and then in a crowd, every woman in the hall stands up and silently raises her right fist.

Notes

NA: Northumberland Archives
ULSC: University of Liverpool Library, Special Collections
WL/LSE: the Women's Library Collection at the LSE Library

1. Designed for happiness

1 M. Royden, *Josephine Butler* (London: Josephine Butler Fellowship, n.d.), p. 1.
2 Professor James Stuart's tribute to Josephine was published in *The Shield* (organ of the repeal movement) in January, 1907.
3 Letter from H. Grey to E. Morrison, 10 Nov. 1849, quoted in G. G. Butler, 'Some Recollections of Josephine Butler', NA ZBU/E/3/E/3.
4 NA, ZBU/E/2/11.
5 J. Jordan, *Josephine Butler* (London: Hambledon Continuum, 2007), p. 28.
6 G. W. and L. A. Johnson, *Josephine Butler* (Bristol: Arrowsmith, 1928), p. 18.
7 This was Josephine's description of the girl, WL/LSE, 3JBL/9/25/21.
8 WL/LSE, 3JBL/9/25/21; M. Ashworth in 'The Englishwoman', vol. 23, issue 67 (1914), p. 38.
9 J. Jordan, *Josephine Butler*, p. 46; WL/LSE, 3JBL/9/25/21.
10 J. Butler, *Recollections of George Butler* (Bristol: Arrowsmith, [1892]), p. 96.
11 M. Fawcett and E. Turner, *Josephine Butler* (London: Association for Moral and Social Hygiene, 1927), p. 29.
12 J. Butler, *Recollections*, p. 98.

2. Campaigns and crusades

1 J. Butler, *Recollections of George Butler* (Bristol: Arrowsmith, [1892]), p. 153. A lost memoir of Josephine by Ralph Butler is

referred to by Margaret Forster in *Significant Sisters* (London: Secker and Warburg, 1984), p. 55; I have also drawn on this.

2 J. Butler, 'Private Thoughts' (manuscript notebook), NA, ZBU/E/3/A/2.

3 J. Butler, *Recollections*, p. 183.

4 E. Hopkins, *The Black Anchor* (London: Hatchard, 1883) p. 14 (copy not seen).

5 J. Jordan, *Josephine Butler* (London: Hambledon Continuum, 2007), p. 81.

6 ULSC, JB 1/1, 3 August 1867.

7 J. Jordan, *Josephine Butler*, p. 74.

8 In 1869, 218 soldiers out of every 1000 were treated for VD. See [M. Fawcett], *Notes for Speakers on the Work and Principles of Josephine Butler* (Westminster: Association for Moral and Social Hygiene, 1928), p. 10.

3. Revolt of the women

1 J. Butler, *The Voice of One Crying in the Wilderness* (Bristol: Arrowsmith, 1913), reprinted in *Josephine Butler and the Prostitution Campaigns*, ed. J. Jordan and I. Sharp (London: Routledge, 2003), vol. 1, p. 32.

2 J. Butler, *Personal Reminiscences* (London: Horace Marshall, 1910), p. 8.

3 J. Butler, *Paper on the Moral Reclaimability of Prostitutes* (London: Ladies' National Association, 1870), p. 7.

4 J. Butler, 'Private Thoughts' (manuscript notebook). NA, ZBU/E/3/A/2.

5 J. Butler, 'The Garrison Towns of Kent. Third Letter from Mrs Butler.' (*The Shield*, 9 May 1870).

6 T, Fisher, 'Josephine Butler' (*History Today*, vol. 46, issue 6, June 1996), p. 34.

7 Florence Nightingale was apt to be peevish about those whose motives she found hard to understand. She once accused the Crimean heroine Mary Seacole of keeping a brothel.

8 J. Butler, 'Species of Diary from June 1890 until April 1895,' typescript, NA, ZBU/E/3/A/12.

9 J, Butler to F. Harrison, 9 May 1868, WL/LSE, 3JBL/2/20.

10 J. Butler, *Personal Reminiscences*, p. 49.

11 J. Butler, *Personal Reminiscences*, p. 50.

12 J. Butler, *Personal Reminiscences*, p. 73.

13 G. W. and L. A. Johnson, *Josephine Butler* (Bristol: Arrowsmith, 1928), p. 90.

14 J. Butler, *Recollections of George Butler* (Bristol: Arrowsmith, [1893]), p. 390.

4. Hard work, but God is good

1 A. Dyer, *The European Slave Trade* (London: Dyer, 1880), p. 4.

2 A. S. G. Butler, *Portrait of Josephine Butler* (London: Faber and Faber, 1954), p. 139.

3 A. S. G. Butler, *Portrait*, p. 142.

4 Henry J. Wilson files, WL/LSE, 3HJW/D/1.

5 E. Riley in *The Southport Visiter* [sic], 3 May 1898, p. 15.

6 A. S. G. Butler, *Portrait*, p. 205.

7 J. Butler to (son) G. G. Butler, 15 February 1895. WL/LSE, JB1/1.

8 A. S. G. Butler to G. G. Butler, 30 December 1906, NA, ZBU/E/3/C/5.

9 R. Butler to G. G. Butler, 2 January 1907, NA, ZBU/E/3/C/5.

10 *The Stormbell*, issue 10 (December 1898). Quoted by A.B. Russell-Jones in her thesis *The Voice of the Outcast* (University of Birmingham, 2015), p. 40.

5. An almost ideal woman

1 F. Forsaith to H. Wilson, 5 January 1907, WL/LSE, 3JBL/52/13.

2 These are now held in Northumberland Archives.

3 NA, ZBU/E/3/C/4/3.

4 NA, ZBU/E/3/C/2/2.

5 W. Stead quoted in *The Berwickshire News and General Advertiser*, 22 January 1907.

6 Reprinted in *The Hampshire Chronicle*, 5 January 1907.

7 *The Hastings and St. Leonards Observer*, 12 January 1907.

8 *The Newcastle Daily Chronicle*, 4 January 1907.

9 [M. Fawcett], *Notes for Speakers on the Work and Principles of Josephine Butler* (Westminster: Association for Moral and Social Hygiene, 1928), p. 13.

10 Special Collections, Leeds University Library, MS 1314, 23916.

6. Portraits in words and pictures

1 These are listed in J. Jordan, *Josephine Butler*, pp. 348-50.

2 J. Butler to F. Forsaith, 5 March 1903, WL/LSE, 3JBL/47/13.

3 J. Butler to unnamed recipient, 25 October 1900, WL/ LSE, JB1/1.

4 J. Butler to E. Morrison, 22 June [1851], quoted in J. Jordan, *Josephine Butler*, p. 29.

5 This was the melancholy portrait chosen to sit in solitary splendour at her memorial function at Westminster's Caxton Hall in April 1907.

6 J. Butler to G. Watts, quoted in a letter to *The Times* from Winifred Coombe Tennant, 7 July 1928, NA, ZBU/E/3/C/2/1.

7. Ignorance is not bliss

1 J. Butler, 'A Woman's Place in Church Work' (*The Independent*, 25 February 1892).

2 J. Butler, *The Lady of Shunem* (London: Horace Marshall, 1894), p. 3.

3 Notes by Charles Grey, NA, ZBU/E/3/C/7/2.

4 A. Neilans writing in *Our Freedom and its Results by Five Women* (London: Hogarth Press, 1936), p. 212.

5 A. Neilans, *Our Freedom*, p. 213.

6 J. Butler, *The Constitution Violated* (Edinburgh: Edmondson and Douglas, 1871), p. 36.

7 J. Butler, *Social Purity* (London: Morgan and Scott, 1879), p. 36.

8. Do not imagine you are powerless

1 In H. Mathers, *Patron Saint of Prostitutes* (Stroud: History Press, 2014) there is a helpful list of the places where Josephine lived throughout her life, pp. 198-200.

2 Quoted in an article in *The Times*, 15 February 1978, by J. Ansell.

3 J. Butler, 'Letter to the International Convention of Women', 1888, p. 19. Photocopy in ULSC, Spec Butler 40.

4 J. Butler, 'Letter', p. 21.

Further reading

By Josephine Butler

It is not easy to find copies of Josephine's works outside scholarly libraries and archives. If you are able to get hold of them, I would recommend *Personal Reminiscences of a Great Crusade*, originally published in 1896 and reprinted in 2012 by <www.forgottenbooks.org>. *Recollections of George Butler* (1892), Josephine's biography of her husband, is enlightening about her own life. The best place to listen to her distinctive voice, however, is in the pages of *Josephine Butler and the Prostitution Campaigns: Diseases of the Body Politic*, edited by Jane Jordan and Ingrid Sharp in five volumes (London: Routledge, 2003). This monumental undertaking reprints much of her output, illuminating her life and times in a unique way.

About Josephine Butler

Where does one start? I consulted some 100 printed sources in the course of researching this brief history – not to mention the manuscript material found in archives. If I were to suggest just a handful, they would be Jane Jordan's *Josephine Butler* (London: John Murray, 2001, reprinted by Hambledon Continuum in 2007); Helen Mathers's *Patron Saint of Prostitutes* (Stroud: History Press, 2014); Josephine's grandson Bob's biography (A. S. G. Butler, *Portrait of Josephine Butler* (London: Faber and Faber, 1954)); Margaret Forster's *Significant Sisters* (London: Secker and Warburg, 1984, reprinted several times); and *Our Freedom and its Results by Five Women* (London: Hogarth Press, 1936). The last two are group biographies, supplying context to Josephine's story.

About the period

For background reading on the CDAs, Judith Walkowitz's book *Prostitution and Victorian Society: Women, Class and the State* (Cambridge: Cambridge University Press, 1980) is excellent. For an understanding of the concurrent campaigns for education and women's suffrage, I can't resist recommending two of my own books: *Bluestockings: the Remarkable Story of the First Women to Fight for an Education* (London: Penguin, 2010) and *Hearts and Minds: the Untold Story of the Great Pilgrimage and How Women Won the Vote* (London: Black Swan, 2019).

Index

Index